Amoris Laetitia

A NEW MOMENTUM for MORAL FORMATION and PASTORAL PRACTICE

EDITED BY GRANT GALLICHO
AND JAMES F. KEENAN, SJ

INTRODUCTION BY
CARDINAL BLASE CUPICH

Paulist Press
New York / Mahwah, NJ

Library of Congress Control Number: 2017964282

ISBN 978-0-8091-5417-3 (paperback)
ISBN 978-1-58768-794-5 (e-book)

Published by Paulist Press
997 Macarthur Boulevard
Mahwah, NJ 07430

www.paulistpress.com

Printed and bound in the
United States of America

To Pope Francis and the Synod of Bishops

Contents

CONTENTS

Contents

Acknowledgments

We want to thank Cardinal Blase Cupich, Fr. William P. Leahy, SJ, and the Jesuit Institute at Boston College, as well as the Healey Family Foundation, Henry Luce Foundation, Inc., and an anonymous donor for their support in hosting the original seminar on *Amoris Laetitia*.

We also express our gratitude to Connor Murphy, Jack McErlean, and Liam Haffey for their editing and Fr. Mark-David Janus, CSP, and Donna Crilly at Paulist Press for their wonderful support in the publication of this collection.

Introduction

Cardinal Blase Cupich

*I*n his address at the celebration of the fiftieth anniversary of the Synod of Bishops, Pope Francis observed that "the Synod of Bishops is only the most evident manifestation of a dynamism of communion that inspires all ecclesial decisions." There are two other levels in which synodality needs to be exercised for the church to be fully an *ecclesia docens* and *ecclesia discens*, a teaching and a learning church.

The first is in the context of a diocesan synod, "in which priests and laity are called to cooperate with the bishop for the good of the whole ecclesial community." The second is the act of synodality that takes place when groups of bishops come together provincially, regionally, or nationally. This intermediate level of episcopal collegiality, the Holy Father remarked, unfortunately has not been realized. In fact, while some bishops have either called for official diocesan synods or other meetings to consult their clergy and laity following the release of the postsynodal apostolic exhortation *Amoris Laetitia*, it occurred to me that the church in the United States could benefit from gatherings of bishops and theologians to unpack this magisterial document, which has so much promise for the pastoral life of the church.

With that in mind, I invited Fr. James Keenan, SJ, director of the Jesuit Institute at Boston College, to collaborate with me in organizing a seminar to that end. While much of the publicity surrounding *Amoris* has focused on chapter 8 and the so-called irregular marriage cases, it was clear to us that the full document needed to be considered as we dealt with the issue of its reception in the multicultural and diverse environment that characterizes the church in the United States. Moreover, we were keen to make sure that the full range of challenges and issues related to marriage and family life covered in *Amoris*, that is, those dealing with the economy, social trends, and so on, would receive attention in our discussion.

The bishops and the theologians universally agreed that our two-day seminar was an exercise in synodality, a walking together in which the church both taught and listened. In fact, in keeping with the counsel of Pope Francis at the start of the 2014 synod, the Boston College participants spoke with candor and boldness, *parrhesia*, but they also listened with humility.

My hope is that this publication of the presentations by bishops and theologians at Boston College will not only introduce readers to the theological depth found in *Amoris Laetitia*, but will also provide a model of synodality, which Pope Francis is calling for in the life of the church, especially as it relates to the interaction between theologians and bishops. Our seminar so very effectively modeled what a synodal church should look like, I believe, because participants were willing to invest in what Pope Francis refers to as *collegialitas affectiva*. Affective collegiality is not a matter of warm feelings and being nice to each other, but, as the Holy Father noted on the occasion of the fiftieth anniversary of the Synod of Bishops, it is an important ingredient in making the ministry of bishops more effective as they join "together with the pope in solicitude for the People of God." Among everything else we learned and shared in Boston, the experience of theologians and bishops working together, affectively and effectively, while not foreseen, was perhaps the most valuable outcome of our time together.

Understanding and Misunderstanding the Scope, the Challenge, and the Promise of *Amoris Laetitia*

1

How Is *Amoris Laetitia* Being Received?

COLONIALISM, CONSCIENCE, AND ACCOMPANIMENT

Natalia Imperatori-Lee

This essay presents some categories within which the reception of *Amoris Laetitia* in the Latino/a community (which I will refer to as Latinx) should be understood. Beyond that, it points to ways that Latinx Catholics, in their lives and through their theologies, stand at the leading edge of a church of encounter and accompaniment, ushering us away from a church of command and obligation. My view of this reception and this contribution necessarily takes a hemispheric perspective, not only because of the technological advances that have shrunk our hemisphere or because of the demographic reality of a predominantly Latinx Catholic Church here in this country, but because popes since John Paul II have encouraged U.S. Catholics to embrace a self-understanding that there is but one *ecclesia* in America. Thus, any discussion of ecclesial reception in America should draw on a hemispheric range of sources. Insights not only from Hispanic theologians in the

United States, but also from theologians in Mexico and in Peru, from Pope Francis's comments in Columbia, the guidelines of the Argentine bishops—these are part of the reception of *Amoris Laetitia*. In addition to the macrocosm of the hemispheric church, my understanding of the reception of *Amoris Laetitia* is informed by the microcosm of my own social location as a married mother of two sons, a laywoman theologian, and a Cuban American. I must confess much of my sense of the impact of *Amoris Laetitia* comes from my experience of coraising two children, particularly the futility and folly of supposing that a family is anything like a closed system where expectations are presented by parents and flawlessly followed by children. Family life has been, for me, an experience marked by *metanoia*, a constant catechesis inviting me to rethink what I presumed were inflexible principles (such as "maternal instinct," or "family expectations") and applying them to the living, evolving relationships in which I am entwined daily. It is my hope that Pope Francis is inviting the whole church into the dynamic that I learn in my own corner of the domestic church. So, within the framework of Francis calling the church to a new catechesis on the family, what do the experiences of Latinx Catholics have to offer to the reception of this postsynodal exhortation?

Three key concepts we must understand to grasp the reception of *Amoris Laetitia* in Latinx communities are colonialism, conscience, and accompaniment. The reception of *Amoris* cannot be understood apart from the historical context of colonialism in Latin America and in Latinx communities in the United States. The legacy of colonialism is one marked by violence: physical, cultural, and spiritual. This legacy means that in the Latinx community, certain dangerous tendencies are intensified in the interaction of families, and laypeople generally, with the church. Ecclesially, this is manifest in two complementary realities: the infantilization of the laity and clericalism. Reading *Amoris* from the perspective of the Latinx church, we see Pope

Francis pointing to the infantilization of laypeople and families that is so commonly a feature of colonization in paragraph 37:

> We have long thought that simply by stressing doctrinal, bioethical and moral issues, without encouraging openness to grace, we were providing sufficient support to families, strengthening the marriage bond and giving meaning to marital life. We find it difficult to present marriage more as a dynamic path to personal development and fulfilment than as a lifelong burden. We also find it hard to make room for the consciences of the faithful, who very often respond as best they can to the Gospel amid their limitations, and are capable of carrying out their own discernment in complex situations. We have been called to form consciences, not to replace them.

The desire to replace the conscience of the laity, or the failure to "make room" for them, points to a vision of the laity as dependent children incapable of higher-order moral thought. Infantilizing the laity in this way has its historical roots in a view of laypeople as objects of clerical control: there to pay, pray, and obey, or as Pius X notes in *Vehemente Nos*, "The one duty of the multitude is to allow themselves to be led, and, like a docile flock, to follow the Pastors" (no. 8).[1] If this was true of the laity broadly understood, it was intensified in the case of colonized territories like Latin America. Historically, non-European cultures were viewed as indolent and incapable of learning, particularly indigenous and black communities. This accounts for the dearth of indigenous clergy all over Latin America for so many years. The repercussions of the dominant culture's reluctance to ordain indigenous clergy can still be seen in the relatively small number of Hispanic bishops in a church that is increasingly Spanish-speaking here in the United States. Thirty-eight percent of U.S. Catholics self-identify as Latinx, yet just 3 percent of priests do.

Within this colonial frame, married life can still be viewed vestigially as a haven for lust, particularly for populations of color in which hypersexuality is assumed as a cultural feature. Conjugal life is therefore overdetermined, an object of moral pronouncements and abstract ideals about the function of marriage as unitive, procreative, indissoluble. Failure to live up to these ideals reinforces the caricatures of indolence, violence, and again, of hypersexuality. In the face of this, we see many marriages in Latinx communities that are irregular: couples circumvent the church because of lack of access to clergy, or circumstances of migration precluding the reality of marriage, or lack of resources to pay for a church wedding, which, though scandalous, remains true.

Laypeople are infantilized further by a logic, pointed out by the Argentine bishops' guidelines on *Amoris*, where pastors serve as gatekeepers offering permission for sacraments, rather than as counselors who accompany Catholics on their sacramental journeys.[2] The gatekeeper paradigm is not limited to Latinx churches, as I learned firsthand at my son's confirmation preparation meeting, during which the pastor of the parochial school declared that he, and he alone, decides who gets confirmed in our neighborhood. In *Amoris*, Francis espouses the imagery of accompaniment rather than gatekeeping, promoting the laity's ability to discern appropriate courses of action.

One could easily come to the facile conclusion that this infantilization of laypeople is a great sin committed only by the clergy. The phenomenon is not one-sided, though. Clericalism is the complement to the infantilizing impulse of the colonial view, and it is not a problem unique to the clergy. Pope Francis's repeated admonitions against clericalism serve as a warning for the laity as much as for priests, maybe even more pointedly for laypeople. Nonclergy are tempted to clericalism, to elevate the priest to superhuman status, and thereby to infantilize themselves: to become children who are told what to do, which can be easier than doing the hard work of developing one's conscience and engaging in discernment. Infantilization and clericalism cannot be separated, nor are they sins that belong only to one sector or another of the church. We are all sinners here.

Against the logic of colonialism, clericalism, and infantilization, we must assert the message of liberation theology, that the poor and the marginalized are subjects of their own history. Analogously, then, the family after *Amoris* becomes the protagonist of its own destiny. In *Amoris* 200, we read that the synod fathers declared that Christian families are the "principal agents of the family apostolate." Couples become the subjects of their history even as pastors and confessors retain a role of accompaniment and listening in order to orient this intrafamilial ministry.

A second category within which to understand the reception of *Amoris Laetitia* in Latinx cultures is conscience. When the document claims, in paragraph 37, that we are called to form and not replace consciences, Peruvian theologian Gregorio Perez de Guereñol comments that the replacement of conscience is "an act of domination,"[3] again colonization. It is an abuse of power. The formation of conscience, on the other hand, is lifegiving ministry, because it loves an other into freedom. Here it might be beneficial to explore the notion of freedom within the church. Many of the misgivings and nervousness about *Amoris* expressed in some sectors of the church seem to surround the move away from doctrine as something one asserts expecting obedience, toward doctrine as something derived from unchanging principles, but that nevertheless requires application to specific circumstances, not all of which are identical. The concern is often expressed in a worry that this will "confuse the faithful," which, yet again, reflects an infantilizing impulse. This move is itself, I fear, a childish view of the freedom necessary for discernment and conscience. Let me give you a real-world example. My children lament that they are not adults, because adults "get to do whatever they want." My standard response, in varying tones, depending on the amount of patience I have remaining (usually very little), is "I never, *ever*, get to do what I want." In moving away from rigid magisterial presentations, some fear that relativism will creep in, that the laity will just "do whatever it wants." This is a child's view of freedom. Adult life, as we all know, particularly adult life enmeshed in relationships of care, seldom results in doing "whatever I want." My desires are always already desires-in-relation. My decisions affect my spouse and children and mother and colleagues and students.

Latinx theology invites us to think of human freedom differently, because it presents an alternate view of the human person. Gary Riebe-Estrella noted that Latinx communities, rather than being voluntary associations of individuals focused on self-determination, tend to view themselves, anthropologically, as socially constituted.[4] This preexistent "we" that characterizes "me" factors in to the reception of *Amoris* in Latinx communities. Reibe-Estrella's description highlights a different approach to the human person shared by many outside of the Latinx community, and serves as an invitation to those who don't: Latinx Catholics have long embraced James Keenan's suggestion that *Amoris Laetitia* proposes relationality in the face of cold rationality.[5] Roberto Goizueta's work builds on this anthropological notion of "we": he describes humanity-in-relation as necessary, preexistent. Entering relationship is not merely an option between two autonomous individuals. There is a sense in which we belong to other people; this is what makes us human. We are responsible to others. Freedom, then, is not freedom from interference, but rather freedom in relation.[6] This freedom is where conscience operates, and it functions in relation, not as an individual act of an isolated will.

The third and final category I wish to highlight in Latinx theology that helps contextualize the reception of *Amoris Laetitia* is accompaniment. No other word speaks to the goal of Pope Francis's papacy and the point of *Amoris Laetitia* like *accompaniment*. It is the praxis that lives alongside conscience, between ideal principles and their application to particular situations, and it is the special vocation of Christians to accompany one another. Accompaniment is a notion at the heart of Latinx communities—in language and expressions of grief (*Te acompaño en tu dolor* / "I accompany you in your pain"), in our greetings and goodbyes (*Que Dios te acompañe* / "May God accompany you"). Deeply rooted in these cultures, it's not surprising that accompaniment features as well in Latinx theology: in Goizueta's *Caminemos con Jesus*, as just one example. A model of ministry, and really an entire ecclesiology based on accompaniment, is what, I believe, Francis is aiming for in *Amoris Laetitia*. This marks, crucially, a move away from what Cardinal Schönborn has called an "ethics of obligation that generates both laxity and rigorism."[7] The ethics of obligation is an ecclesiological hallmark of North American Catholicism, influenced by Northern European cultures. Latinx theologians like Goizueta suggest accompaniment as an alternative model rooted in the popular Catholic practices of a variety of Latinx cultures. The act of traveling-with an other is seen in devotions like Christmas *posadas* or Marian devotion to the Virgen Dolorosa or to Nuestra Señora de la Soledad. For Goizueta, accompaniment guards against romanticization, because we can only romanticize that which we do not truly know.[8] What does this accompaniment look like in *Amoris Laetitia*? The walking-with families and couples traversing diverse realities and true challenges serves as a catechesis for all the companions on the journey. Just as popular Catholic practices in Latinx communities foreground the sacred in the everyday, accompaniment in ministry may reveal the possibility that the daily life of couples and families has something to offer doctrinal pronouncements on marriage. If nothing else, accompaniment works against the romanticization of marriage and family that pervades our church's teaching on these topics, and even creeps into *Amoris* in its discussion of mothering and fathering in chapter 5. Accompaniment implies equality, a walk alongside demands empathy and understanding from all parties, but it also implies ethics and politics: in what direction are we walking?[9] This is, for Goizueta, a central concern, and the point for understanding Francis's exhortation is that it must not be the theologian or the pastor alone who sets the direction. The magnetic north of accompaniment is the encounter with Christ. The fact that ethics is involved in accompaniment does not automatically assign the role of directing or navigating to the pastor. Rather, everyone on the journey is capable and called to navigate, and there will be times (as there have been) when couples lead the way to the encounter with Christ. It is possible, then, for pastors accompanying families to learn that couples themselves are able to point toward this encounter with God, and invite the whole church to learn from this. If we learn nothing else from Latinx theology, we should know that the sacredness of the everyday is paramount, the scandal of the incarnation is that this right here, this messiness, this ugliness, is where grace can be found. Accompaniment allows us to affirm everyday particularity and embodiment in its beauty and its ugliness, and this is the model of family ministry to which the postsynodal exhortation invites us.

In truth, there is no way to speak for the 30.4 million Hispanic Catholics in the United States or for their reception of *Amoris Laetitia*. As a systematic theologian, I can point to specific problems that certainly resonated with these communities: the pervasive reality of domestic violence, the horror of drug addiction and alcohol abuse in families, and the impact of unjust migration laws and abject poverty on couples. I can also highlight ways in which the message of *Amoris* is intensified by the colonial history of Latin America and the United States, the violence of clericalism, and the infantilization of the laity in which we all participate. But the takeaway should not be the ways the Latinx community is reacting to the document, but rather the varied ways in which Latinos/as, in their daily lives and practices, and in their theological and anthropological insights, invite all Christians to embody the message of *Amoris* in the church universal. The centrality of conscience and freedom-in-relation, the notion of relationality as a preexistent condition of humanity and not an act of the will, and the vision of accompaniment as a model for ministry in all aspects of the church are what I hope will be the contributions of the reception of *Amoris* in this country, and indeed the whole church.

NOTES

1. See http://w2.vatican.va/content/pius-x/en/encyclicals/documents/hf_p-x_enc_11021906_vehementer-nos.html.

2. The letter can be accessed in Spanish at http://www.infocatolica.com/?t=ic&cod=27336. The first point reads, "We should recall that one should not speak of 'permission' to receive the sacraments, but rather of a process of discernment accompanied by a pastor" [translation mine].

3. Gregorio Perez de Guereñu, "*Amoris laetitia* y madurez humana y ecclesial," *Páginas* 244 (December 2016): 26–34. "Sustituir la conciencia del otro es, en definitive, dominarla, domesticarla, imponer una determinada forma de ivda, con lo que nuevamente caemos en el error de tomar al laidco como un menor de edad que necesita ser llevado de la mano porque personalmente no es capaz de hacer su propio camino" (30).

4. See Gary Reibe-Estrella, "Pueblo and Church," in *From the Heart of Our People: Latino/a Explorations in Catholic Systematic Theology* (Maryknoll, NY: Orbis Books, 1999), 172–88.

5. See Keenan's "Receiving Amoris Laetitia," in *Theological Studies* 78, no. 1 (March 2017): 193–212.

6. For Goizueta's understanding of freedom-in-relation, see *Caminemos Con Jesús: Toward a Hispanic/Latino Theology of Accompaniment* (Maryknoll, NY: Orbis Books, 1995), esp. chap. 3.

7. Antonio Spadaro and Christoph Schönborn, "Cardinal Schönborn on 'The Joy of Love': The Full Conversation," *America* Magazine, August 9, 2017, at https://www.americamagazine.org/issue/richness-love.

8. Goizueta, *Caminemos Con Jesús*, 193.

9. Goizueta, *Caminemos Con Jesús*, 219.

2

How Is *Amoris Laetitia* Being Received?

AMORIS LAETITIA AND THE BLACK CATHOLIC COMMUNITY

C. Vanessa White

Pope Francis's apostolic exhortation *Amoris Laetitia: The Joy of Love* acknowledges the challenges facing families today and addresses the pastoral implications for ministers who journey with families.

I am grateful for the opportunity to share this reflection on how *Amoris Laetitia* has been received within the black Catholic community in the United States. As a womanist practical theologian whose focus is spirituality and ministry, I wish to begin by framing my remarks with the words and experiences of a diverse community of black Catholic scholars, theologians, and ministers.

I acknowledge the contributions of first-generation black Catholic theologians[1]—M. Shawn Copeland, Diana Hayes, and Jamie T. Phelps—as well as the work of a black Catholic historian, Fr. Cyprian Davis, whose book *History of Black Catholics in the United States* has given voice to black Catholics whose contributions and history had remained invisible within the institutional church. Of further note is the work of moral theologian and activist Fr. Bryan Massingale, whose ground-breaking book *Racial Justice and the Catholic Church* is must reading for anyone ministering here in the United States. The writings of Copeland, Hayes, Phelps, Davis, and Massingale are an invaluable resource for gaining a greater understanding of the context of black Catholic faith, life, and spirituality.

The late Cyprian Davis writes that the story of African American Catholicism is the story of a people who obstinately clung to a faith that gave them sustenance, even when it did not always make them feel welcome.[2] I share with you a reflection from a black Catholic graduate of Catholic Theological Union: titled "Like a Motherless Child," it addresses the reality of black Catholics, who experienced hostility and isolation within a church that did not readily acknowledge their gifts or presence.

Like a Motherless Child[3]

Mother Church. I am here.
Mother Church I am ready.
Mother Church I am willing.
Mother Church, I have been knocking for years,
You have locked me out for years,
I will not go away.
I will not disappear.
You have to open your doors.
I will not stop knocking.
Mother Church, I will knock till there is a hole in
    your door.
I will come through the hole.
I will bring my open heart and my open mind.
I will bring my mother, my God.
Yes, Mother Church, I am here.
I am knocking, I am willing, I am ready,
I will no longer feel like a "Motherless Child."

Black Catholics had to fight for their faith, and this fight was not only with other Catholics (who questioned their legitimacy as Catholics) but often with members of their own household who could not understand why they embraced a faith that did not always recognize their gifts. Black Catholic families challenged one another and challenged the church to be truly Christian and Catholic. Who are black Catholic families?

In the book *Families: Black and Catholic, Catholic and Black*, Sr. Thea Bowman states that within African American households can be found "large families, small families, nuclear families, extended families, single-parent families, adopted and foster families, rich families, poor families, matriarchal and patriarchal families, inner city, central city, rural city, gospel loving, happy, healthy, rich, poor, working, jobless, shouting, testifying, fussing, and fighting families."[4] There is not one typical description that can be ascribed to African American families. Psychologist Andrew Billingsley shares that black families stretch beyond the confining depiction of husband and wife with two children and instead are a multiple variety of nuclear, extended, and augmented family forms that have survived because of their strength, endurance, adaptability, resilience, and faith.[5]

In 2011, sociologists Darren Davis and Don Pope-Davis hoped to shed a light on the faith of African Americans in the first ever National Black Catholic Survey, sponsored by the National Black Catholic Congress and the Institute for Church Life at the University of Notre Dame. This survey sought to measure the religious engagement of African Americans. Davis and Pope Davis concluded from their study that African American Catholics tended to be highly engaged, particularly if they were members of a predominately black parish. Membership in a black parish reflects shared social and cultural experiences that connect people through a common identity.[6] The importance of social connections of African American Catholics and the influence on religious engagement cannot be overstated.

This would tend to reinforce what our black bishops initially stated in 1984, in their pastoral letter on evangelization in the black community titled *What We Have Seen and Heard*. In this letter, the bishops recognized four characteristics of black spirituality and religiosity. Black spirituality is "contemplative, holistic, communitarian, joyful."[7] Furthermore, for black Catholics, God was felt "Deep Down in Their Souls,"[8] and, as Sr. Thea Bowman has stated, their spirituality is the "Soul of the People."[9] To minister to African American Catholic families, one must understand the roots of their spirituality and how their spirituality has shaped their family life and culture.

These findings support the work and focus of African American Catholic marriage and family-life ministers Andrew and Terri Lyke. For the past thirty-five years, the Lykes have focused on marriage and family within the black community with their Arusi Network ministries, and addressed the importance of attending to the spirituality and culture of African Americans in responding to the needs of families. In their new book, *Marriage on a Lampstand: Exploring a New Paradigm for Modern Christian Marriage*, they have sadly concluded that the institution of marriage has virtually collapsed among African Americans. As the Lykes have shared, "We marry least compared to all measured ethnic groups and when we marry, we divorce at the highest rate."[10] What has been the Catholic Church's response?

According to the Lykes, predominately African American parishes are the least likely to have viable marriage-outreach programs. This is disturbing, considering the challenges that face black Catholic families today. Within the African American family today, there is a virtual litany of challenges: racism, depression, unemployment, underemployment, police brutality, domestic abuse, layoffs, systematic exclusion from full participation in political, educational, economic, and religious institutions, violence, incarceration, lack of resources, and so forth.[11] In light of these challenges, what new approaches to catechizing, encouraging, supporting, and celebrating marriage have been implemented? An African proverb holds, "It takes a village to raise a child." While many in the black community affirm these words, in today's context of mobility and increased individualism, it does not direct our current actions or "shape our protocols for how we relate to one another as parishioners, neighbors, and community members."[12] In light of the challenges within black families today and the increased isolation experienced by many families in urban settings, Terry and Andrew challenged pastoral ministers and pastoral leadership to consider the following question: Are we reaching out to those who are ambivalent about marriage, yet are forming families? *Amoris Laetitia* addresses this question:

> We live in a culture which pressures young people not to start a family, because they lack possibilities for the future....We need to find the right language, arguments and forms of witness that can help us reach the hearts of young people, appealing to their capacity for generosity, commitment love and even heroism and in this way inviting them to take up the challenge of marriage with enthusiasm and courage. (no. 40)

Andrew Lyke states that *Amoris Laetitia* invites and empowers an expansive approach to the church's accompaniment of families regarding the sacrament of marriage. In their new book, they focus on the document's approach to accompaniment of families. For the Lykes, a major theme of *Amoris Laetitia* is accompaniment, which is addressed in chapter 8. As pastoral leaders, we must walk with families and assist in restoring hope. They state that there is a symbiotic relationship between marriage and community and the ministry of accompaniment that leads couples, regardless of their marital status, to participate in the sacramental life of the church through the public witness of marriage.[13]

While *Amoris Laetitia* seeks to address the reality and challenges of family life, unfortunately this document has not had an impact in the life of the black Catholic community. When I was asked to give this presentation, I informally solicited feedback from colleagues in the black Catholic community (i.e., members of the Black Catholic Theological Symposium, black Catholic graduate students at Catholic Theological Union, and ministers in the black Catholic community). Most responded that the impact has been primarily indistinct.

At the same time, one response was striking and came from a black Catholic director of religious education whose ministry focuses on families in a predominately black Catholic parish. The question I posed to her was, "How has *Amoris Laetitia* been received in the black Catholic Community?" She responded,

> When *Amoris Laetitia* first came out, it was discussed briefly and we included information in flyers, but there wasn't an overall interest from the congregation to read the document in its entirety. Some of our families are in survival mode, struggling with under- and unemployment, divorce, and single parenthood. Families are simply trying to ensure that their children are not victims of the violence that plagues our city [Chicago]. We have families that come to church occasionally because of the struggles they are facing. If it is a question of work, school, or church, some of our families choose the former rather than the latter.[14]

She continued,

> While the pope's words are encouraging and provide guidelines for ministers to serve God's people, our families are looking for more tangible solutions that plague them. I would say that rather than just talking about the *Joy of Love* as a document, we who have read it are attempting to use it as a guide to provide the support that our families need. This is in the form of journeying with parents and children when they are faced with struggles, providing them with resources

that can help them, and letting them know that the church and Eucharist are always there to nourish their bodies and souls without restrictions. I guess by letting our families know that they are not alone in the struggle and that God has not forsaken them, that is the best way we can implement the *Joy of Love*.[15]

Her response sheds light on how *Amoris Laetitia* must be in dialogue with the life and context of the people. Church leadership in the United States must learn and continue to make strides to understand the current reality of black people. I am reminded of the story of Jesus and the Samaritan woman at the well (John 4:4–28). Jesus knew her context, he responded and affirmed her gifts, he took the time to be present to her, and she was transformed. We must address the current realities of the black community, which has been challenged historically and in the present day by racism that has institutionally taken forms of increased unemployment and underemployment, inadequate health, incarceration, increased violence in our communities, and so on. These all impact families. As Jesus knew the context of those he ministered to, we must do the same if we wish to have spiritual and pastoral impact in the black community. Our families are suffering because we have not addressed their pain, their reality, or their struggles. If *Amoris Laetitia* is to have a lasting impact on black Catholic families, pastoral leaders must show how the exhortation and the church itself address the challenges of black Catholic family life, acknowledge the gifts and spirituality of the people, and give hope to the future generations of black Catholics. The selected bibliography is a step in that direction as we continue to journey together in the days ahead to minister to families from our diverse communities and to truly live out the hopes and goals of *Amoris Laetitia*.

NOTES

1. M. Shawn Copeland, *Enfleshing Freedom: Body, Race, and Being* (Minneapolis: Fortress Press, 2009); Diana Hayes, *Standing in the Shoes My Mother Made: A Womanist Theology* (Minneapolis: Fortress Press, 2010); Jamie T. Phelps, *Black and Catholic: The Challenge and Gift of Black Folk* (Milwaukee: Marquette University Press, 1997); and Bryan Massingale, *Racial Justice and the Catholic Church* (New York: Orbis Books, 2010) are excellent resources for understanding the context of black Catholic life.

2. Cyprian Davis, *History of Black Catholics in the United States* (New York: Crossroad, 1990), 259.

3. Mary Norfleet Johnson, "Like a Motherless Child," in *Songs of Our Hearts and Meditations of Our Souls: Prayers for Black Catholics*, ed. Cecilia Moore, C. Vanessa White, and Paul M. Marshall (Cincinnati: Franciscan Media, 2006), 56. All rights reserved. Used with permission of the publisher. The African American spiritual "Like a Motherless Child" is source material for this reflection.

4. Thea Bowman, *Families: Black and Catholic, Catholic and Black* (Washington, DC: United States Catholic Conference Commission on Marriage and Family Life, 1985), 20.

5. Andrew Billingsley, "When We Think of Family...," in Bowman, *Families*, 21.

6. Darren W. Davis and Donald B. Pope-Davis, *2011 National Black Catholic Survey* (National Black Catholic Congress and University of Notre Dame Institute for Church Life, 2011), 31.

7. Joseph L. Howze, Harold R. Perry, and Eugene A. Marino, et al., *"What We Have Seen and Heard": A Pastoral Letter on Evangelization from the Black Bishops of the United States* (Cincinnati: St. Anthony Messenger Press, 1984), 8–11.

8. Experience of God that has been orally transmitted from generation to generation within the black community.

9. Thea Bowman, *Sister Thea Bowman, Shooting Star: Selected Writings and Speeches*, ed. Celestine Cepress (La Crosse,

WI: Franciscan Sisters of Perpetual Adoration, 1999), 38. Originally published as "Spirituality: The Soul of the People," in *Tell It Like It Is: A Black Catholic Perspective on Christian Education* (Oakland, CA: National Black Sisters Conference, 1983), 84–85.

10. Paula Goodwin, Brittany McGill, and Anjani Chandra, "Who Marries and When? Age at First Marriage in the United States 2002," Data Brief No. 19 (Hyattsville, MD: U.S. Department of Health and Human Services, Centers for Disease Control and Prevention, National Center for Health Statistics, June 2009), https://www.cdc.gov/nchs/products/databriefs/db19.htm.

11. Thea Bowman, "The Challenges," in *Families*, 32.

12. Andrew Lyke and Terri Lyke, *Marriage on a Lampstand: Exploring a New Paradigm for Modern Christian Marriage* (Alpharetta, GA: Visual Dynamics Publishing, 2017), 48.

13. Interview with Andrew Lyke, September 29, 2017.

14. Interview with T.C., director of religious education (DRE) in the Archdiocese of Chicago, September 29, 2017.

15. Interview with T.C., DRE in the Archdiocese of Chicago, September 29, 2017.

SELECTED BIBLIOGRAPHY

Executive Committee of the Black Catholic Theological Symposium (BCTS) in collaboration with the Board of Directors of the Academy of Catholic Hispanic Theologians of the United States (ACHTUS). *ACHTUS/BCTS Statement Regarding the Most Recent Surge in Racist Hate Crimes in the United States*. September 4, 2017. http://bcts.org/ and http://www.achtus.us/.

Black Catholic Bishops of the United States. *What We Have Seen and Heard*. Pastoral Letter on Evangelization in the Black Catholic Community. Washington, DC: USCCB, 1984.

Bowman, Thea, ed. *Families: Black and Catholic, Catholic and Black*. United States Catholic Conference. Publication No. 890–98. Washington, DC, 1985.

Davis, Darren W., and Donald B. Pope-Davis. *2011 National Black Catholic Survey*. National Black Catholic Congress and University of Notre Dame. 2011.

Lyke, Andrew, and Terrie Lyke. *Marriage on a Lampstand: Exploring a New Paradigm for Modern Christian Marriage.* Alpharetta, GA: Visual Dynamics Publishing, 2017.

McWilliam, Terrie. *Black Pain: It Just Looks Like We Are Not Hurting.* New York: Scribner, 2008.

National Black Catholic Congress. *A Balm in Gilead: The African American Family-Programs for Parish Implementation.* 1992.

White, C. Vanessa, Cecilia A. Moore, and Paul Marshall. *Songs of Our Hearts and Meditations of Our Souls: Prayers for Black Catholics.* Cincinnati: St. Anthony Messenger Press, 2006.

3

How Is *Amoris Laetitia* Being Received?

Fr. Louis J. Cameli

*E*ven before responding to the question of how *Amoris Laetitia* (AL) is being received in our U.S. context with all its cultural and religious diversity, we need to consider two prior questions: Is it being read? And how is it being read? I cannot provide hard statistics. But relying on sample conversations with priests, ecclesial lay ministers, and laity in general, I conclude that nearly all of them have not read *Amoris* or, if they have, it has been in a cursory way. In general, people know *Amoris* through secondary sources that focus almost exclusively on chapter 8, "Accompanying, Discerning and Integrating Weakness," and, within that, the question of divorced and remarried Catholics and their admission to the Eucharist. Of course, that is a question and a concern of great importance for some people, and it ought to be for the church at large. But *Amoris* has a much, much larger scope, challenge, and promise than that.

At the beginning of the document, Pope Francis acknowledges the difficulty of reading his text. He writes, "Given the rich fruits of the two-year Synod process, this Exhortation will treat, in different ways, a wide variety of questions. This explains its inevitable length. Consequently, I do not recommend a rushed reading of the text" (no. 7). In addition to the challenging length of the document, its patterns of organization and development can also prove to be challenging. So, Cardinal Francesco Coccopalmerio, in his commentary on chapter 8, reordered the themes to make more evident what he calls the "logic of the arguments."

Whether because of its length or internal organization, *Amoris* is not easy to read. As I noted, most people have not read it but instead have relied on secondary reporting, with its often uneven presentations. And for those who do read it, it becomes, in effect, something of an ecclesiastical Rorschach test: people project their own concerns or perspectives on the text, whether those have to do with doctrine, morality, juridical questions, or pastoral practice. All this is understandable, but it is also unfortunate, because *AL* breaks new and important ground for the life of the church and the future of faith. Certainly, elements of doctrine, morality, law, and pastoral practice are present in *Amoris*, especially as presuppositions. But the whole of it—what Italians would call the *insieme*, the whole of it together—is nothing short of a new momentum for spiritual-moral formation and pastoral practice, as the title of our conference indicates. In a word, *Amoris* is a formation document, and that is what makes it both remarkable and novel in the tradition of magisterial teaching. This novelty, as I hope to illustrate, has its roots in the Second Vatican Council, with the Council's concern for human experience and for the journey of the pilgrim people of God. *Amoris* takes those concerns and situates marriage and family life as a central focus for conversion and transformation in the Christian life. In a sense, this movement is a logical consequence of the spiritual revolution begun by St. Thérèse of Lisieux and her foundations for a democratization of holiness, that is, an immediate and full access to holiness for all people in the ordinary circumstances of their lives.

Perhaps on first hearing, these affirmations do not seem to be exceptional in any particular way. In fact, unlike any other magisterial document that I know of, as a document of Christian formation, it sets a context to move from human experience to the spiritual transformation of that experience and those who hold it. In other words, *Amoris* engages those who are married and in family life in a way that can foster growth in their lives as disciples of Jesus empowered by the Spirit, ultimately leading them to the perfection or full actuation of their love.

As I read *AL* with a "formational lens," I detect four drivers in its composition and development that move from experience to experience transformed. The first driver is for married people and families to claim their experience with all its lights and shadows. The second is to see the experience in the light of the gospel. The third is to hear a call to conversion. And, finally, the fourth is to carry that transformed experience to a world deeply in need. When I read *Amoris* with these four drivers in mind, what initially seemed to me to be a long and lumbering text achieved a deep coherence and a compelling argument.

The roots for *AL* as a document of formation rest in the Second Vatican Council, more specifically, in at least three important proposals of the Council: the universal call to holiness, the importance of dialogue in an *ecclesia discens et docens*, and the journey or process dimension of the Christian life for individuals and the entire community as the pilgrim people of God.

Let me repeat, we are not accustomed to a magisterial document that is formational, especially in the context of marriage and family life. If you consult Edward Schillebeeckx's classic two-volume study *Marriage: Human Reality and Saving Mystery*, you can understand that for most of the first two millennia, the theological and magisterial developments around marriage and family life had mainly to do with juridical questions and the theological question of the sacramentality of marriage. Only in the past two centuries, with the crisis of family life triggered by the industrial revolution and then the availability of artificial contraception, do the teachings on marriage

24

shift, but then mainly to resolve questions of rights and morality. Even Pope John Paul II's exhortation *Familiaris Consortio* (1981) is fundamentally a reprise of questions around doctrine, rights, morality, social analysis, and pastoral care.

Amoris Laetitia, on the other hand, assumes doctrine, moral teaching, law, and basic pastoral care concerning marriage and family life. There are no changes, despite claims to the contrary, for example, in the *sic dicta dubia*. *Amoris Laetitia* does offer spiritual and moral formation by helping and preparing people to live out their commitment as disciples of Jesus Christ and to grow in it in the context of marriage and family life. So, it assumes that the Christian life unfolds in a process, that it has real ideals that remain even when we vary in reaching them, and that neither programs nor pronouncements but God's grace leads us forward, although we, with God's help, can create those favorable conditions for accepting that grace.

As a magisterial document that serves the spiritual and moral formation of the people of God, *AL* is unique. Were we to search for parallels, two strong examples from our spiritual tradition would come to my mind: *The Rule of Saint Benedict* and *The Spiritual Exercises of Saint Ignatius*. Both of these precious resources from our tradition situate disciples of Jesus in a particular environment—whether of community life or a meditative-contemplative experience of the Gospels—with the goal of opening believers to transformation either as *conversatio morum*, a full conversion of life, or *a new freedom to act from love and find God in all things*. Formation in this context never means stamping out Christians in cookie-cutter fashion. It means attention to the concrete and particular, the unique and unrepeatable story of this individual, this marriage, and this family.

Finally, let me say that the famous chapter 8 that deals with irregular situations does not look the same when you view it from the perspective of formation. It does not deviate from doctrinal or moral teaching. And Fr. Basilio Petra, president of the Italian Association of Moral Theologians, has unequivocally demonstrated in his commentary *Amoris laetitia: accompagnare, discernere e integrare la fragilita* that the practical directives in chapter 8 echo the classical *praxis confessorum*, confessional practice, that one might find in St. Alphonsus Maria de Liguori in one form or another.

In the end, *AL* is waiting to be read and then received as a remarkable path of spiritual and moral formation for ordinary people living extraordinary lives in marriage and family. That, in my estimation, sums up the scope, the challenge, and the promise of *AL*. And so, in the words Augustine heard in the moment he sought God's grace and God's grace sought him, we can begin by saying to each other and to those we serve, *Tolle, lege!*

4

How Is *Amoris Laetitia* Being Received?

MERCY AND *AMORIS LAETITIA*: INSIGHTS FROM SECULAR LAW[1]

Cathleen Kaveny

INTRODUCTION

*T*he goal of this set of essays is to look at how *Amoris Laetitia* (*AL*) has been received by diverse perspectives, communities, and constituencies.[2] The diversity that I bring to the conversation does not pertain to my background, but instead to my professional expertise: in addition to being a moral theologian, I am also an American lawyer and law professor.

Many people think of law—both secular law and canon law—as an abstract and abstruse set of arbitrary commands. In their view, the law may be useful in enforcing moral norms, but it can never give us moral perspective, or prompt us to develop new moral insights. In my judgment, however, this view of law is incorrect or, at the very least, highly inadequate. Precisely because the law is forced to deal with concrete cases and situations, it is often called to address questions that more abstract reflections on human action and the common good can glide by or avoid. It cannot avoid grappling with the nitty-gritty of moral life. As strange as it may sound, I believe the law— canon law and secular law—can be an ally of Pope Francis's call for renewed attention to concrete human experience.

Does the secular law, in particular, have anything to teach us about mercy? I want to suggest that it does. In so doing, I will be bringing insights from secular law into conversation with some of the controversy swirling around chapter 8 of *AL*, especially the conditions under which the divorced and remarried may receive communion, which is the focus of footnote 351 in the document. Before proceeding, a caveat is in order. Much ink, both real ink in newspapers and virtual ink in the blogosphere, has been spilled on the question of communion for those who have entered second marriages without obtaining a church annulment. An overarching goal of this conference has been to broaden the discussion to encompass *AL* in its entirety, not merely to revisit its most controversial passages. Nonetheless, chapter 8 is part of the document, and I hope that my own expertise may shed some light on the controversy.

CARDINAL KASPER'S INSIGHT

One of the most articulate collaborators with Pope Francis's approach in *AL* has been Cardinal Walter Kasper, who has written movingly about the theological roots and ecclesiological imperative of the virtue of mercy.[3] In a lecture on "The Gospel of the Family," Kasper applies his thoughts about the relationship of mercy, justice, and law to questions such as how the church deals with the question of communion for divorced and remarried individuals.[4]

Kasper makes his case with a passionate rhetorical point: "If forgiveness is possible for the murderer, then it is also possible for the adulterer."[5] That point rings true to many people's experiences and sensibilities. Murder is much worse than adultery. If a repentant murderer can go to communion, why can't someone who has repented of the harm caused by and through his or her disastrous first marriage and gone on to conduct a fruitful, life-giving second marriage also receive the sacrament of the Eucharist?

But those opposed to infusing flexibility into the current rule against giving communion to divorced and civilly remarried persons have a ready response to Kasper's comparison and query: they point out that no one is worthy to receive the Eucharist who has *any* unrepented and unforgiven mortal sin on his or her conscience. But all sins can be repented and forgiven through the sacrament of reconciliation. However horrible, the murder is a *completed* wrong—it is over and finished. Consequently, the murderer can repent of her wrongdoing, which is in the past. She can go to confession, repent her sin, and receive absolution. The situation of divorced and civilly remarried persons is different. Such persons are engaged in a *continuing* pattern of the mortal sin of adultery, at least as long as they continue to have conjugal relations with their second spouse. Because they intend to continue sleeping with their second spouse, they do not have the firm purpose of amendment. Consequently, they cannot be absolved of their adultery. Because they have not received absolution, they are not worthy to receive communion.

This seems like watertight logic. But is it? Is there a way to break out of this frame? I would like to suggest that we might turn to the secular criminal law for some inspiration about how to reframe the problem. More specifically, I think that the criminal law can help us reflect on three issues that seem to underlie the debate about footnote 351.[6] These include the following: (1) How, exactly, do we number and count wrongful acts? (2) How do we determine when a wrongful act begins and when it ends? (3) How does a commitment to mercy affect the way we address the first two questions?

NUMBERING AND COUNTING WRONGFUL ACTS

As I described previously, the core of the critical response to Cardinal Kasper's interpretation of *AL* is the claim that parties to a second civil marriage cannot receive communion because they are continually committing the wrongful act of adultery. But what, exactly, is the definition of the adulterous act those parties are committing? Drawing on Pope John Paul II's encyclical *Familiaris Consortio*,[7] some suggest that the adultery involved in the second marriage comprises every act of sexual intercourse between the parties to that marriage. But is that true? Is it necessary or even conceptually adequate to conceptualize their "adultery" as a series of discrete acts that correspond to each of their sexual encounters? Here, the experience of the criminal law in numbering and counting offenses may offer some helpful insights. Part of the task of the criminal law, after all, is to describe and count offenses with some precision.

More specifically, the first task facing any prosecutor is to determine the "unit of prosecution" for the wrong committed by the defendant. This task is not always easy. Does a thief who takes six gold coins off one bedroom vanity table commit one crime or six? Does a teacher who punches a child three times commit one crime or three? The challenge in defining the crime is more difficult when what is at stake is not merely an isolated action, but instead an organized pattern of behavior. For example, one might ask whether the crime of operating an illegal tavern is one offense, or if the offenses mount up with every drink poured or customer served.

Secular courts have had no choice but to grapple with these questions. Most interestingly, American courts have had to confront them in the context of sexuality and marriage because of the legal challenges presented by the Mormon commitment to polygamous marriage in the nineteenth century.[8] The federal government's opposition to polygamy was unyielding; lawmakers and judges saw themselves as defending the Christian model of marriage (and the dignity of women) against licentiousness and female subjugation. Moreover, and more relevant to our purposes, is the fact that they treated Mormon polygamy as a cover for a pattern of unlawful cohabitation and adultery—in much the same way that those opposed to Cardinal Kapser's approach treat civil divorce and remarriage today. Consequently, the manner in which nineteenth-century federal courts assessed and counted these offenses against monogamous Christian marriage may shed some light on how Catholic moralists and canonists ought to conceptualize the situation of the divorced and remarried in our own community today.

Consider, for example, the case *In re Snow* (1887).[9] Lorenzo Snow was a polygamist living in Utah. The federal prosecutor charged him with three counts of unlawful cohabitation for three successive calendar years. The Supreme Court of the United States held that the federal government could not arbitrarily divide a single, uninterrupted, three-year, unlawful cohabitation into three separate criminal charges; the description of the crime needed to conform to the lived reality of the defendant. Consequently, the court decided that he should be charged with *one* count of unlawful cohabitation.

In a second case, *In re Nielsen* (1889),[10] the federal government charged Hans Nielsen with unlawful cohabitation and the separate crime of adultery. Rejecting the government's way of framing Nielsen's criminal activity, the U.S. Supreme Court held that adultery was a *lesser crime included within the crime of cohabitation.* Significantly, the court looked at the big picture: it recognized that the problem raised by the Mormon polygamy cases was not only, or mainly, the sex outside the first marriage considered in the abstract. For the American legal system and the values that it was committed to uphold, the fundamental problem was the fact that Mormon men falsely understood themselves as entering an additional marital relationship—an additional whole-life partnership of which the sexual acts were only one part.

31

It seems to me that the experience of the U.S. courts in dealing with polygamy could assist the church in understanding the situation of divorced and remarried persons today. From a moral perspective, the proper description of their activity is committed cohabitation. It is a gross distortion of reality to portray a civilly divorced and remarried Catholic as engaged in multiple, disconnected acts of adultery. The parties to the second marriage are not skulking off to a hotel room to grasp a moment of irresponsible pleasure. They are engaged in an ongoing, committed, undivided, and organized life project, which includes but is not limited to sexual relations. If there is a wrong against the first marriage, that second life project is the primary offense; the sexual activity is best conceptualized as a "lesser included offense."

An unavoidable corollary of my argument is that however well-intentioned, Pope John Paul II's approach to the question of communion for the divorced and remarried is significantly misguided. *In re Nielsen* helps us to pinpoint the fundamental flaw in his approach. While *Familiaris Consortio* required the parties to a second marriage to live together as brother and sister, it did not demand that they break up their household. They could be absolved of their sin of adultery if they refrained from further sexual relations. In my view, this pastoral solution rests upon a highly contestable understanding of marriage in that it implicitly denies that the entire relationship between a married couple is shaped by the erotic and conjugal bond between them. In a nutshell, it problematically suggests that being married is not that different from being friends with benefits.

THE BEGINNING AND ENDING OF WRONGFUL ACTS

If we really ponder the crime of murder in all its concreteness, the idea that it is over nearly instantaneously is quite incredible. The searing pain lasts as long as the lives of those who loved the victim. The harm to the common fabric lasts at least as long as the victim would have lived. So the courts distinguish between the criminal *act*, which is over in a finite amount of time, and the *effects*, which may continue indefinitely.[11]

One might respond that the distinction is easily and obviously drawn by looking at the physical world: the defendant's offense (act or omission) defines the scope of the criminal act, what happens after that offense is over should be counted as its effects. Yet the distinction between a criminal act and its effects is not simply a distinction drawn by observation; it also has a significant normative component. Consider, for example, the case of *Toussie v. United States* (1970).[12] Robert Toussie was legally required to register for the draft within five days of his eighteenth birthday, which occurred in 1959. He never registered with a draft board at any time, even though the law required every American man aged eighteen to twenty-six to do so. Toussie was criminally indicted for draft evasion in 1967 and subsequently convicted of that crime. He argued on appeal that the indictment was barred by the five-year statute of limitations.

The case turned on when the crime of draft evasion was completed, because the statute of limitations does not begin to run until that point in time. Toussie maintained that the crime was complete five days after his eighteenth birthday—in 1959. Consequently, the statute of limitations would bar any prosecution beginning five days after his birthday in 1964. But the U.S. government countered that the crime continued every day that Toussie did not register until he reached the age of twenty-six—in 1967. In the government's view, therefore, the statute of limitations would not bar prosecution until 1972.

The U.S. Supreme Court sided with Toussie, and reversed his conviction. The court set out a two-pronged test to identify continuing crimes. First, courts are to look at the intention of the lawmaker: does the legislature intend to define the wrong as a continuing wrong or not? Second, courts are to look at the nature of the crime. The key factor here is whether the offense features "a harm that lasts as long as that course of conduct persists." The hallmark of the continuing offense is that it

33

endures beyond the initial illegal act, and that "each day brings a renewed threat of the evil [the lawmaker]" even after the elements necessary to establish the crime have occurred." At the same time, the courts have recognized that even "continuing offenses do not, in general, continue indefinitely."

Some casuistry is helpful in getting a fuller picture of the complications involved. Not surprisingly, the paradigm of a continuing offense is kidnapping—it is not treated as a completed offense until the victim is released or dies (in which case a new crime of homicide may arise). Yet bank fraud is not generally perceived as a continuing offense, even if it involves maintenance activity on the part of the offender. In *U.S. v. De La Mata* (2001),[13] the defendants had entered a number of fraudulent lease agreements. They collected payment on the leases until the police caught them. When did their crime actually end? The prosecution maintained that the defendants were engaged in a continuing offense that did not terminate until they were caught. The court disagreed: "Taken to its logical conclusion, the collection of rents on a lease obtained by fraud, for a term of 99 years, would toll the statute of limitations for 99 years. We think this goes too far." From the court's perspective, the criminal act was completed when the leases were signed. Collecting the rents was conceptualized not as part of the criminal act, but rather as part of the effects of the crime.

In my view, the secular law on continuing offenses offers lessons that can be applied by analogy to the situation of divorced and remarried Catholics in two ways. First, in deciding whether an offense meets the technical legal definition of a continuing offense, the courts focus on whether the harm that the law is designed to prevent continues to mount up throughout time in a way that can be effectively addressed through the law. Let us assume for the sake of argument that a divorced person who has remarried has inflicted some wrong upon their first marriage. Is it correct, really, to say that the harm to the original spouse, their children, and the community, continues to pile up indefinitely, year upon year? In most cases, it seems to me that this is not an accurate depiction. The harm is completed with the dissolution of the first marriage, and all that it entails, such as the separation of one household into two households. One could argue that the second marriage ceremony causes some additional harm, as it is a definitive sign that the first marriage has no realistic chance of being revivified. But the lethal harm done to the first marriage is completed when the second marriage ceremony takes place.

Second, the case law suggests that we might do well to adopt the distinction between the offense itself, on the one hand, and living out the effects or consequences of the event, on the other. We don't need to treat the sexually active couple in a second marriage as continuing the offense. The life of the second marriage, including its sexual relationship, is best seen as a living out of the second wedding ceremony, which in most cases decisively ends the possibility of the resumption of the first marriage. In other words, the situation of the second marriage is more like the bank fraud case than the kidnapping case.

MERCY AND REPOSE

My brief foray into criminal law shows, I think, that decisions about how to individuate and count wrongful acts are not self-evident or straightforward. Neither are decisions about when a wrongful act itself comes to an end. Both types of decisions implicate various values and policies of the legal system that makes them. In the American legal system, one of these values, the value of repose, bears resonances of the role that places in the thought of Cardinal Kasper and Pope Francis. Legal scholar Jeffrey Boles defines *repose* as consisting of the "interrelated concepts of affording peace of mind, avoiding the disruption of settled expectations, and reducing uncertainty about the future in the lives of defendants."[14] Apart from the most serious crimes, such as murder, the passage of time significantly qualifies the practice of justice. Charging a middle-aged man with a theft he committed as a teenager undermines the value of repose; it also serves neither justice nor mercy. The legal insight is also a theological one: as Cardinal Kasper has suggested, the value of mercy focuses upon enabling wrongdoers to have a second chance, a new life.[15] That new life is not meant to be solitary. Pope Francis has emphasized that the virtue of mercy should be exercised so that everyone can "participate actively in the life of the community" (*Misericordia et Misera* 14).[16]

The secular value of repose, and its theological analogue in the virtue of mercy, can prompt us to rethink how we conceptualize the wrong committed by a civilly divorced and remarried person. I have argued that it is not true to human experience to frame that wrong as the commission of multiple discrete counts of adultery extending indefinitely throughout the second marriage. It does not reflect the moral and practical realities involved in divorce and remarriage. Instead, I made two suggestions. First, I proposed that we might reconceptualize the wrong done by the second marriage as a decision for committed cohabitation inconsistent with the first marriage. Second, I suggested that we distinguish between the completed wrongful act, on the one hand, and its ongoing effects, on the other. More specifically, I proposed that the wrong against the first marriage is very likely complete with the second wedding ceremony. The living out of that ceremony in a second marriage is not a continuous pattern of wrongdoing, but rather the ongoing effects of a completed wrongful act. Just as we allow a murderer to repent of her crime even though the effects of her crime are ongoing, so we should allow a person who contracts a second civil marriage to repent of her offense against the first marriage, despite the fact that the effects of her wrong may be ongoing as well. If a party to a second marriage can effectively repent of her wrongful act, she may be absolved of her sin and return to communion.

CONCLUSION

Jesus disfavored adultery. Jesus clearly rejects divorce and remarriage as contrary to the original will of God. He clearly treats a man's divorce and remarriage as akin to adultery, and from the earliest times in the Christian community, that judgment has been extended to a woman's divorce and remarriage. But nothing in Jesus's words or conduct demands that the sin involved in divorce and remarriage must be treated as a sin that continues indefinitely, without possibility of effective repentance as long as one's first spouse is still alive. To impose such a requirement in every case is not merciful, and mercy is the ultimate touchstone for the divine lawgiver. We do not need to disturb Jesus's central teaching in order to refine and develop its application in ways that believers have done from the earliest days of the body of Christ.

NOTES

1. This essay crystalizes and condenses reflections I have published in other venues, including *Ethics at the Edges of Law: Christian Moralists and American Legal Thought* (New York: Oxford University Press, 2018), chap. 8; "Mercy, Justice, and Law: Can Legal Concepts Help Foster New Life?" in *Marriage and Family: Relics of the Past or Promise of the Future?* ed. George Augustin (Mahwah, NJ: Paulist Press, 2015), 75–106; and "Mercy for the Remarried: What the Church Can Learn from Civil Law," *Commonweal*, August 14, 2015.

2. Pope Francis, *Amoris Laetitia*, apostolic exhortation, "Love in the Family," 2016.

3. Walter Kasper, *Mercy: The Essence of the Gospel and the Key to Christian Life*, trans. William Madges (New York: Paulist Press, 2013).

4. Walter Kasper, *The Gospel of the Family* (New York: Paulist Press, 2014). This is his lecture to the extraordinary consistory of cardinals on the topic of family life, which took place February 20–21, 2014, in Vatican City.

5. Ibid., 32.

6. My discussion of the secular legal issues is deeply indebted to two articles: William H. Theis, "The Double Jeopardy Defense and Multiple Prosecutions for Conspiracy," *Southern Methodist*

University Law Review 49, no. 2 (1996): 269–307; and Jeffrey M. Chemerinsky, "Counting Offenses," *Duke Law Journal* 58, no. 4 (2009): 709–46.

7. Pope John Paul II, *Familiaris Consortio*, apostolic exhortation, "The Role of the Christian Family in the Modern World," 1981, no. 84.

8. For a fascinating overview, see Sarah Barringer Gordon, *The Mormon Question: Polygamy and Constitutional Conflict in Nineteenth Century America* (Chapel Hill: University of North Carolina Press, 2002).

9. *In re Snow*, 120 U.S. 274 (1887); see Theis, "The Double Jeopardy Defense," 280–81.

10. *In re Nielsen*, 131 U.S. 176 (1889); see Theis, "The Double Jeopardy Defense," 280–81.

11. See the helpful analysis in Jeffrey R. Boles, "Easing the Tension between Statutes of Limitations and the Continuing Offense Doctrine," *Northwestern Journal of Law and Social Policy* 7, no. 2 (2012): 219–56. I am deeply indebted to his article both for his own insights and his valuable collection of sources and citations.

12. *Toussie v. United States*, 397 U.S. 112 (1970).

13. *United States v. De La Mata*, 266 F.3d 1275 (11th Cir. 2001).

14. Boles, "Easing the Tension," 225.

15. Kasper, *Mercy*, 83.

16. Pope Francis, *Misericordia et Misera*, apostolic letter at the conclusion of the Extraordinary Jubilee of Mercy, 2016.

PANEL II

The Novelty That Priests and People Face When They Receive *Amoris Laetitia*

5

Amoris Laetitia in Priestly and Seminary Formation

LIKELIHOOD OF RECEPTION

Sr. Katarina Schuth, OSF

The question presented for this chapter is, "How will the novelty, the newness, and inspiration of *Amoris Laetitia* play out in priestly and seminary formation?" The content of the document ought to be a fundamental element in preparation for ministry since the formation process is important, if not determinative, in how the document will be received by seminarians and then passed on in many other circumstances over time to a variety of church members and groups. I propose this position because of the reality that many, if not most, practicing Catholics come to understand their faith mainly through homilies and other parish involvements and presentations. The essence of what future priests will teach and preach depends on what they learn about the many issues related to family life in *Amoris Laetitia*, including how to encourage laity to engage in discussion of the contents and give input and leadership in its dissemination. That substance and those attitudes will shape to a great extent the realization of the great outcomes hoped for and sought after in parishes and other ministerial settings.

Since laypeople have firsthand knowledge and experience of the struggles and joys of family life, one of the main goals of formation must be to learn how to engage the Catholic community in conversations about *Amoris Laetitia*. This engagement, affirmed in the document, involves listening, accompanying, discerning, and evangelizing.[1] These four activities require knowledge and expertise. Seminary faculty members are unequally prepared to teach the process, and seminarians are unequally willing to embrace the process. The result is that reception and dissemination of *Amoris Laetita* will differ from one seminary to another. Broadly speaking, two outcomes are possible: some participants will engage in all four dimensions, but many will have the tendency to move past the first three directly to evangelizing. In its richest sense, of course, the latter involves the other three activities, but it does not mean catechizing in only the narrowest sense of "instructing (someone) in the principles of the Catholic faith by means of questions and answers."[2]

For many seminarians, therein is the difficulty with *Amoris Laetitia*; it is decidedly *not* a series of answers to questions about the many concerns and struggles of family life, especially those dealing with sexuality and marriage. Rather, it is the challenge of learning how to accompany the faithful by engaging with them in discussion of their concerns and enabling them to discern what is right, that is, helping them to form their consciences relative to these important issues. From my thirty years of engagement with seminaries and seminarians, I believe this process will be difficult for some seminarians and their mentors—but not all of them—to accept. It is necessary to emphasize the fact that reception of the document, or failure to receive it, will not be the same in all cases and places. What are some possible reasons for resistance or acceptance? I will mention the backgrounds of seminarians, the positions taken by faculty, and the expectations of bishops and religious superiors of seminary formation as contributing factors.

First, the religious and educational backgrounds of seminarians have a significant impact. Those who might have problems with implementing the teachings of *Amoris Laetitia* are of several types, of which I offer two examples. First are those who enter seminary with minimal knowledge of their faith. Often some of these seminarians have participated quite minimally in church services and activities, while others are relatively recent converts with minimal conversance with the particulars of church beliefs and practices. Their faith might be described as, at best, a mile wide and an inch deep. They know a little bit about many (and sometimes not so many) essentials of the Catholic Church. Understandably, their desire is to collect *answers*, learning by rote as much Catholic doctrine as they can retain. This task looms large for those who, in a few years, will be leaders of parish communities. Their desire is for knowledge that is clear and certain, indisputable and unquestionable. Development of doctrine generally is not a topic of great interest to them.

The second type are those who come to seminary having practiced their faith in devout Catholic families, sometimes home-schooled, usually in relationships with other young people of like mind who are equally committed and seldom challenged in their faith. At best, this foundation can be a useful beginning for seminary studies. The difficulty comes when their knowledge is in fact an inch wide and a mile deep, that is, they know a great deal about the church from a limited point of view. It leads to a belief that everything about their faith is clear and flawless, well-defined and sure, and thus needs no discussion. Unlike their peers who are not in seminary and are not highly committed to the church and the practice of their faith, seminarians are, of course, deeply involved and committed.[3] Their patience with the necessary engagement in the required process for implementing *Amoris Laetitia* through listening, discerning, accompanying, and evangelizing may be somewhat limited if they expect others to hold the same certainty about all of the church's teachings.

In each case, the presence or absence of certain virtues and qualities that seminarians possess make an enormous difference in their ability to disseminate the content of *Amoris Laetitia*. Those who succeed will have confidence in their ability to converse with parishioners about difficult issues and encourage them to share their experiences; they will have not only deep academic understanding of the topic, but also freedom to engage and be challenged, questioned, and confronted. Acceptance of the viewpoint that the faithful have a right to freedom of conscience is difficult for those who are fearful that they will misrepresent the church's teaching, or more likely, if they hold the position that discussion is impossible or unnecessary since there is only one way to interpret an issue.[4] In the first instance, resistance comes from worry about their own inadequacy, and in the second, the problem may be rigidity. Acceptance will be easier for those with knowledge and heart, compassion and openness to the real lives of people who are allowed to grow toward adherence to church teachings, rather than expecting them to be perfect here and now.

The goal of seminary formation should be to prepare priests who are both confident and open. The task is different for each type of student, but the goal is the same—to enable the seminarian to listen, accompany, and discern the faith with those they will encounter in ministry. That goal involves not only intellectual acuity, but also human, spiritual, and pastoral formation. Each dimension is influential in the challenges of learning to pastor in the mode of *Amoris Laetitia*. This endeavor involves all the "new pieces" identified as needing exploration in the introductory statement for this panel—forming an adult faith, examining the joys and difficulties of marriage and family, understanding the role of conscience, and taking responsibility for decisions. It certainly requires faculty who will help seminarians form an adult faith of their own, deal with the untidiness of discipleship, and accept the role of conscience in the Christian life.[5]

This leads to the faculty, the second set of key participants in the formation process. Two related questions guide the discussion: How are faculty themselves likely to under-stand and appreciate *Amoris Laetitia*? And what guides the approaches they will adopt?

In recent years, the faculty composition in seminaries has been transformed. A large cohort, those educated in the years following shortly after Vatican II, have retired. Only a handful of current faculty were even young adults at the time of Vatican II, and many of their professors in graduate schools were edu-cated largely during the pontificate of John Paul II. This profile makes a difference in the methodologies and approaches used by each cohort, especially in areas of systematic theology, moral theology, and pastoral theology and practice—all of which can affect their comfort with *Amoris Laetitia*. Like students, faculty differ considerably. Some engage subject matter by expanding the learning experience with the goal of instilling freedom and confidence in students to take responsibility for their own view-points. Others are more comfortable with teaching content in a fashion that provides clear answers to students, but does not allow for much discussion or appraisal that suggests the pos-sibility of differing interpretations. Seminarians tend to take on the viewpoints of their teachers, which they carry with them to their ministry once ordained.

Guiding the perspectives of faculty are church documents, some universal, and others, such as the U.S. *Program of Priestly Formation* (PPF), are specific to each country—all composed by bishops and religious superiors. In the United States, five edi-tions of the *PPF* have been published and the sixth is in prepa-ration. If one uses citations as the criterion for distinguishing differences, the first three were most influenced by the docu-ments of Vatican II, the fourth by John Paul II's *Pastores Dabo Vobis* in 1992, and the fifth by canon law in 2005. The focus of the content and methods of each edition shifted consider-ably. Gradually, notions of listening, dialoguing, and discussing seem to have been superseded by the precise answers supplied in large part by canon law. Expansive inclusion of lay faculty and lay students was replaced with focused attention on priests and seminarians. The importance of each iteration of the *PPF* cannot be underestimated in the ways seminaries transform their programs.

The bishops and religious superiors who are responsible for their own seminaries have a great impact on programs by making clear their expectations and preferences regarding the focus of the documents that describe content of formation and how it is provided. Some are more likely to embrace the ideal of educating future priests with an emphasis on a didactic approach that emphasizes fidelity to the magisterium, while others favor an approach that focuses on the spirit of pastoral charity and an openness to serve all people. Both are present, of course, but the level of discussion and interpretation will not be the same with each type. Notable also is the level of support for *Amoris Laetitia* indicated by the bishops and religious superiors in charge of seminaries and their directives in how much the document should be stressed. Considerable variation among them and between diocesan and religious seminaries is evident, based in part on the mission to be served by the graduates.

Obviously, each component—students, faculty, and those responsible for the direction of seminaries—needs more explanation. The major point is that *Amoris Laetitia* will be received and disseminated through priestly and seminary formation programs with greater or lesser enthusiasm depending on many factors. Even within each seminary univocal acceptance will not be experienced. Pope Francis acknowledges how much he has learned from the bishops as they shared their hopes and aspirations, their concerns and challenges during the synod. He said that "the Synod process allowed for an examination of the situation of families in today's world, and thus for a broader vision and a renewed awareness of the importance of marriage and the family" (no. 2). To the extent that priestly and seminary formation makes the teachings of this document an integral part of the program, the more likely will the renewal and rebirth of the church be realized as families feel welcomed and accepted for who they are.

NOTES

1. In a lecture on "Pope Francis, Synodality and *Amoris Laetitia*" (Georgetown University, Washington, DC, Sacred Lecture Series, September 12, 2017), Cardinal Donald Wuerl described this process in detail.

2. The broad sense of catechesis involves the lifelong effort of forming people into being witnesses to Christ and opening their hearts to the spiritual transformation given by the Holy Spirit. See www.usccb.org/about/evangelization-and-catechesis/index.cfm.

3. The book *American Catholics Today*, by William D'Antonio, James Davidson, Dean Hoge, and Mary Gautier (Lanham, MD: Rowman & Littlefield, 2007), 18–19, reports on detailed measures of the strength of Catholic identity. The millennial generation displays the weakest results, with only 7 percent highly committed. The study, updated in 2011 by D'Antonio, shows similar results (though slightly improved); it is found at http://www.ncronline.org/news/survey-reveals-generation-shift-catholic-church.

4. Pope Francis addresses the concern in *Amoris Laetitia* 37: "We have long thought that simply by stressing doctrinal, bioethical and moral issues, without encouraging openness to grace, we were providing sufficient support to families, strengthening the marriage bond and giving meaning to marital life. We find it difficult to present marriage more as a dynamic path to personal development and fulfilment than as a lifelong burden. We also find it hard to make room for the consciences of the faithful, who very often respond as best they can to the Gospel amid their limitations, and are capable of carrying out their own discernment in complex situations. We have been called to form consciences, not to replace them."

5. Pope Francis supports this position, in *Amoris Laetitia* 308, by quoting *Evangelii Gaudium* 270. He says that Jesus "expects us to stop looking for those personal or communal niches which shelter us from the maelstrom of human misfortune, and instead to enter into the reality of other people's lives and to know the power of tenderness. Whenever we do so, our lives become wonderfully complicated."

6

How Is This Newness Read by Canon Lawyers?

Msgr. John A. Alesandro

*P*rocess: **Norms versus Theological Meaning.** For many canon lawyers, *Amoris Laetitia* was not viewed as the most innovative development of the synodal process. It was canonically upstaged by the pope's promulgation, prior to the October 2015 synod, of a major simplification of the process for declarations of invalidity in the Latin and Eastern Churches.[1]

Some canon lawyers are fearful of those norms, particularly the novelty of a *processus brevior* in which the diocesan bishop is, *mirabili dictu*, treated as the chief judge—which, of course, he is. At last year's annual meeting, a group brashly proposed that the Canon Law Society of America recommend that the U.S. bishops delay the implementation of the norms, a resolution that was forthrightly defeated by the assembly. In fact, this role of the diocesan bishop was strongly emphasized by the 2015 synod fathers[2] and *Amoris Laetitia* itself.[3]

The Meaning of Christian Marriage. Process is important, but the real challenge lies in the substance of marriage law: specifically, what qualifies as Christian marriage. Mining the wealth of insights in *Amoris Laetitia* and implementing them requires the invaluable help of theologians. Yet, *Amoris Laetitia* does offer canon lawyers some clues and directions for development.

Tradition with a Twist. On the surface, the document presents a fairly traditional view of marriage, early on distinguishing marriage from de facto or same-sex unions and offering a familiar summation about matrimony later on in chapter 8. In both references, however, there are subtle clues to the development *Amoris Laetitia* is emphasizing: the difference between ideal and practice, between full realization of the ideal and partial.[4] The interplay between *the ideal*—the "newness" that Christ brought to marriage—and *realization* (i.e., making "real") of that "newness" in the individual marriage is extremely important for canon lawyers who are dealing day-to-day with "realization"—either premarriage or in tribunal cases.

Inductive Approach. Canon law lies at the descriptive end of Bernard Lonergan's functional specialties, a kind of "practical theology" and a form of "theological communication."[5] Dealing with real-life couples, canon lawyers are challenged by *Amoris Laetitia*'s inductive approach to maintain two forces in tension: the cultural experience of contemporary marriage and the mystery of Christ in which marriage is immersed.[6] *Amoris Laetitia* implicitly alerts them to hold onto the concrete: do not reduce the specific marriage itself to a cookie-cutter replica of a principle. There is more to mystery than that.

Invalid Marriage. That tension, of course, is intense. Pope Francis and Cardinal Gerhard Müller, former prefect of the Congregation for the Doctrine of the Faith, approach the meaning of marriage along different paths. Yet both have concluded that in the real world, many, if not most, marriages, though presumptively valid in law, are canonically invalid.[7]

Discernment. *Amoris Laetitia*'s emphasis on "pastoral discernment," a challenge one might associate initially with confessors and pastoral ministers, applies equally to tribunal judges, who must make a determination about the individual marriage, guided by sacramental meaning and yet immersed deeply in the details. Even if a specific judgment may not qualify as a general principle, it can still be pastorally discerned as a morally certain decision of nullity in a particular case.[8]

An Example: Relative Incapacity. For example, canon lawyers in the past flirted with the idea of "relative incapacity" as a ground of nullity. Most shied away from it as too similar to the secular notion of "incompatibility." Yet, we claim that the unitive property of marriage (c. 1056) requires the two spouses to be "capable" of becoming one—not one with everyone in the whole world, but specifically with one another. Marriage does not exist in the abstract; it exists only in the individual couple, and *Amoris Laetitia*'s analysis of cultural "individualism" raises this ground again: Even if the two individuals before us are capable of marrying someone, are they really capable of marrying *one another*?

Realization versus Legalization. *Amoris Laetitia*'s inductive approach also counteracts a "creeping legalization" of canon law that is endemic to practitioners. Lawyers like to turn principles (e.g., grounds of nullity) into figurative "boxes" within which the concrete either fits or does not fit. We can construe the facts as far as possible to make them fit, but one never tampers with the frame of the box. (Who knows? Perhaps theologians and pastoral ministers are subject to the same temptation!) *Amoris Laetitia* is reminding canon lawyers that, while that may be workable in a positive law system, marriage is part of the Christ event. You can never "box in" the mystery of Christ.[9] To avoid such legalization, *Amoris Laetitia* does not start conceptually with an abstract definition of marriage nor even with "natural marriage" onto which is grafted the elements of sacramentality and indissolubility. Instead, it identifies the "newness" of marriage in Christ as the norm—in other words, the "full realization" in contradistinction to "partial realization."[10] How does this make a difference for canon lawyers?

An Example: Due Discretion and Sacramentality. Most tribunal judges treat the due discretion required of spouses (c. 1095 §§2–3) identically the same for sacramental and nonsacramental marriages. In a sense, the expert psychiatrist and the judge are supposed to be "baptism-blind" about psychological capacity. Yet, the synodal view suggests that a superior capacity and resolve of the will is required of those entering sacramental marriage than of those entering a nonsacramental union (which is canonically susceptible to dissolution).[11]

Domestic Church. A corollary of this distinction lies in the synodal concept of domestic church. The newness of Christian marriage implies the *capacity of the spouses* and their *resolve* to undertake the vocation of becoming a *domestic church*.[12] In preparing couples and deciding nullities, we do not simply study whether the couples are intending marriage per se, but whether they are *capable of* and *intending*, at least implicitly, to form a domestic church. In short, spouses must have "capacity for the newness of marriage" to enter the covenant validly and a "willingness to bring about that newness" as the proper ministers of the sacrament of matrimony.[13]

Faith. This approach raises for canon lawyers the perennial question with which the International Theological Commission, recent popes, and the Roman Rota have struggled: the import of faith on marital consent.[14] To use traditional terminology, the "newness" of Christian marriage affects the *matrimonium in fieri* as well as the *matrimonium in facto esse*. It is not enough for the baptized to consent to a valid "natural" marriage; there is more to it if they are to become sacramentally, and therefore validly, "one flesh"—that is, caught up in the mystery of Christ. Some have suggested that sacramentality simply *happens* to spouses because they are baptized (even if they do not know it). My reading of the synodal teaching is that the marriage's sacramentality is a *necessary element* of their capacity, intention, and will. Another way of putting this is that truly "marital" consent is not posited in a vacuum to which is attached the object of the consent, which *happens* to be marriage—and for the baptized, *happens* to be a *sacramental* marriage.[15]

Marriage Preparation. In that regard, the final synodal reports and *Amoris Laetitia* are excellent tools for premarriage preparation. Pope Francis's meditation alone on the key words of the thirteenth chapter of Paul's First Letter to the Corinthians would be an excellent tool for them to prepare spiritually and realistically for their loving commitment to each other.

Foresight and Hindsight. *Amoris Laetitia* presents another challenge to canon lawyers: do not draw too great a distinction in your approach to marriage preparation and to causes of nullity. Before the wedding, it seems eminently advisable to try our very best to foster the ideals of Christian marriage in our engaged couples. We know that they cannot yet absorb everything but—meeting them where they are—we sincerely trust that we will be able to help these two spouses sufficiently. But when it comes to making a retrospective judgment about a broken marriage in a tribunal case, some canon lawyers settle for "traditional" abstract grounds of nullity and rules of evidence—an approach that unfortunately may shortchange the ideal of Christian marriage as the true standard of validity. The reality of marriage presented by *Amoris Laetitia* applies in both directions: going forward into marriage and looking back at the results. The ideal is the norm; the individual marriage is the realization or nonrealization or possibly partial realization of it.

A Time of Development in the Grounds. The science of canon law undergoes cycles: periods of development, followed by times of stasis. *Amoris Laetitia,* I believe, is initiating for canon lawyers a time of development, akin to the tremendous insights and applications that occurred in the twentieth century regarding due discretion and the capacity to assume the obligations of marriage—a development that started with concrete cases in the first instance, worked its way into decisions of the Roman Rota, and, with the help of the conciliar documents, found a home in the Codes of Canon Law (c. 1095 and CCEO 818).

Beyond Psychology. *Amoris Laetitia* crystalizes a call to go beyond psychological diagnoses about natural marital capacity and to apply what we have learned to the paradigm of marriage in the New Dispensation, a paradigm that calls for more in the engaged couple's commitment to such a vocation. For example, *Amoris Laetitia*'s view of marital maturity as a process[16] goes far beyond the Diagnostic and Statistical Manual of Mental Disorders definition of the "Immature Personality Disorder."[17] Tribunal judges are challenged to recognize in individuals, even without a clinical diagnosis, a marital immaturity that truly made them incapable of positing specifically Christian marital consent.[18]

Technology and Truth. Sometimes incapacity will emerge from the phenomenon Pope Francis terms as "technological disconnect."[19] Tribunals are seeing more and more the "Google generation," members of whom understand truth as available at the click of a keypad, and for whom commitment to the enduring journey of marriage "does not compute."

Sexuality. All of this is of course caught up in the deleterious effect that contemporary tendencies about sexuality have on marital capacity. Sexuality is "trivialized and impoverished." It is not set "within the broader framework of an education for love, for mutual self-giving," the very essence of marital consent (*AL* 280).

In the end, the novelty of *Amoris Laetitia* requires canon lawyers to recognize religious or pastoral grounds of nullity that are deeper than purely psychological incapacity. They are reasons why the individual marriage may fall short of sacramentality and absolute indissolubility, the norm of Christian marriage.

Conjugal Love. All of this is summarized in the challenge for canon lawyers to take Christian conjugal love seriously. Specifically, Christian love is the core of the marriage bond itself (*matrimonium in facto esse*) and—a crucial point for canon lawyers—the root of the covenantal process by which spouses enter marriage (*matrimonium in fieri*). Canon lawyers may find it difficult to get their juridical minds around "love" if their thinking has become overly "legal" (which is another way of saying "secularized")—but they are supposed to be practical theologians, not simply jurists.[20]

Tenderness. For example, *Amoris Laetitia* insists that conjugal love is necessarily marked by tenderness.[21] It is not a nicety; it is essential to the sacrament of marriage. *Amoris Laetitia* is challenging judges in a tribunal process to discover, in the concrete, whether both spouses (including the man) were, at the time of the wedding, truly capable of tenderness in the sense described by Pope Francis—the tenderness of a mother cradling her infant.[22]

Paul and Love. Francis's masterly analysis of chapter 13 of 1 Corinthians is not simply a tool for marriage preparation. It offers concrete guidance about the conjugal love that must be ingrained in the spouses in order to give themselves to each other by marital consent and to live out that consent. The synodal experience is calling on canon lawyers to take the words seriously as the constitutional makeup of the spouses and irreplaceable building blocks of a valid sacramental covenant.[23]

Journey. A corollary to this view is "marriage as journey," which is prevalent throughout *Amoris Laetitia*. Spouses must be capable of entering a lifelong adventure and able to renew it constantly if they are to exchange consent validly.[24] Christian love requires them to be "friends on the journey." While they do not start out whole and complete, they must at least be *able to grow* into their vocation. If spouses are incapable of that growth, their commitment fails to rise to the level of *caritas*; it remains simply barter and invalid—a less than full realization of what Christian marriage is.[25]

"Sacramentalization." Perhaps I am reading too much into it, but it seems to me that *Amoris Laetitia* as a whole supports quite nicely the idea that, in time, sacramental marriages become "more sacramental," and therefore "more indissoluble." It may be a very short time or an extended journey. For some, however, although they begin marriage, they never achieve the "sacramentalization" that captures the newness of the Christ event in marriage.

Sacramental versus Natural. The key to appreciating such an approach is theological: refusing to identify a sacramental marriage simplistically with a valid natural marriage of spouses who happen to be validly baptized (as c. 1055 §2 insists). A true breakthrough would be to admit that sacramentalization is a vocational process that starts with valid marital consent and reaches its essential completion (or, as Gratian termed it, "consummation") at a point that one can only reasonably determine by hindsight. It is not "all or nothing."

To me this would make sense of our pastoral efforts: (1) trying our best to prepare couples, knowing that they are just starting out, rather than putting them through a sacramental wringer (sort of a marital RCIA); (2) trying to help couples who are struggling, to see if they can get back on the right track, without suggesting that they are not validly married; (3) granting declarations of the invalidity not only of marital consent but of the marriage's sacramentality (full realization); and finally, (4) when circumstances warrant, allowing such determinations to occur in the internal forum.

NOTES

1. *Motu proprio Mitis Iudex Dominus Iesus* for the Latin Church and *Mitis et Misericors Iesus* for the Eastern Churches, both effective on December 8, 2015. Process is dear to the heart of all lawyers, civil and canonical, who are cognizant of the veiled truth in the old adage: "If the law is on your side, argue the law. If the law is not on your side, argue the facts. If neither the law nor the facts are on your side, argue procedure."

2. "The implementation of these documents is therefore a great responsibility for Ordinaries in dioceses, who are called upon to judge some cases themselves and, in every case, to ensure the faithful an easier access to justice." *Relatio Finalis 2015* 82. See *Amoris Laetitia* 244.

3. "The bishop himself, in the church over which he has been appointed shepherd and head, is by that very fact the judge of those faithful entrusted to his care," *motu proprio Mitis Iudex Dominus Iesus* (August 15, 2015) Preamble, III (*L'Osservatore Romano* [September 9, 2015], 3).

4. Marriage has "a plenary role to play in society as a stable commitment that bears fruit in new life" and de facto or same-sex

unions "may not simply be equated with marriage" for they cannot "ensure the future of society." "Only the exclusive and indissoluble union between a man and a woman has a plenary role to play in society as a stable commitment that bears fruit in new life...de facto or same-sex unions, for example, may not simply be equated with marriage. No union that is temporary or closed to the transmission of life can ensure the future of society" (*AL* 52). The union of Christ and his church is "fully realized" in Christian marriage. Some unions "radically contradict this ideal, while others realize it in at least a partial and analogous way." "Christian marriage, as a reflection of the union between Christ and his Church, is fully realized in the union between a man and a woman who give themselves to each other in a free, faithful and exclusive love, who belong to each other until death and are open to the transmission of life, and are consecrated by the sacrament, which grants them the grace to become a domestic church and a leaven of new life for society. Some forms of union radically contradict this ideal, while others realize it in at least a partial and analogous way" (no. 292).

5. Canon law is "a form of *theological communication*— i.e., the application of a doctrinal system faithful to the revelation of Christ insofar as this revelation has been understood systematically in history." See J. Alesandro, "Implementing Church Law—A Theological Specialty," *CLSA Proceedings*, October 13–16, 1986 (Washington, DC: CLSA, 1987), 334–43, at 338.

6. As Fr. Francis Morrisey has stated, "Instead of starting with principles, and working its way down to practical situations, it begins with situations to see how best they can be addressed in the light of certain principles." F. Morrisey, "Some Pastoral Implications Arising from Chapter VIII of the Apostolic Exhortation *Amoris Laetitia*," *The Canon Law Society of Great Britain and Ireland Newsletter* (June 2016), 53–80, at 53.

7. It is not easy for the "ideal" to be "fully realized," at least as the church's "ideal" is canonically constructed. Addressing Rome's pastoral congress this past June, Pope Francis, in responding to a question about the crisis in marriage, mentioned "the culture of the provisional" as a reason that "the great majority of our sacramental marriages are null. Because they say 'yes, for the rest of my life!' but they don't know what they are saying. Because they have a different culture. They say it, they have

good will, but they don't know." This comment was later officially amended to read "a portion of our sacramental marriages are null." (Catholic News Agency, "Updated: Most Marriages Today Are Invalid, Pope Francis Suggests," June 16, 2016, http://www .catholicnewsagency.com/news/most-marriages-today-are-invalid -pope-francis-suggests-51752/).

Similarly, Cardinal Gerhard Ludwig Müller notes, "Marriages nowadays are probably invalid more often than they were previously, because there is a lack of desire for marriage in accordance with Catholic teaching, and there is too little socialization within an environment of faith." Müller, "Divorced and Remarried," *L'Osservatore Romano* (October 23, 2013), Eng. transl. Vatican Radio in Zenit.org (October 24, 2013).

8. In another text, referring to the general knowledge of the rule and the particular knowledge of practical discernment, St. Thomas states that "if only one of the two is present, it is preferable that it be the knowledge of the particular reality, which is closer to the act." *Sententia libri ethicorum*, VI, 6 (ed. Leonina, t. XLVII, 354.). See *Amoris Laetitia* 348.

9. Otherwise, you end up presenting, as *Amoris Laetitia* states, "a far too abstract and almost artificial theological ideal of marriage, far removed from the concrete situations and practical possibilities of real families" (no. 36).

10. Francis cites Alexander of Hales to support the notion that in a certain sense marriage should be considered superior to the other sacraments (*AL* 159) because it specifically symbolizes the great reality of "Christ's union with the church, or the union of his divine and human natures." Alexander of Hales, *Glossa in quatuor libros sententiarum Petri Lombardi*, IV, XXVI, 2 (Quaracchi, 1957), 446.

11. This view is fortified by the comparison of marriage as a vocation to consecrated virginity. "Whereas virginity is an 'eschatological' sign of the risen Christ, marriage is a 'historical' sign for us living in this world, a sign of the earthly Christ who chose to become one with us and gave himself up for us even to shedding his blood. Virginity and marriage are, and must be, different ways of loving" (*AL* 161).

12. Jesus "assumes human love and brings it to fulfillment. By his Spirit, he gives spouses the capacity to live that love, permeating

every part of their lives of faith, hope and charity. In this way, the spouses are consecrated and by means of a special grace build up the Body of Christ and form a domestic church (cf. *Lumen gentium*, no. 11), so that the church, in order fully to understand her mystery, looks to the Christian family, which manifests her in a real way" (*Relatio Finalis 2014* 17). See *Amoris Laetitia* 67.

13. Francis points out that for "baptized persons, the commitment expressed by the words of consent and the bodily union that consummates the marriage can only be seen as signs of the covenantal love and union between the incarnate Son of God and his Church" (*AL* 213).

14. Quoting John Paul II, *Amoris Laetitia* sees the commitment of the spouses as an eloquent language of faith, "the language of the ministers of the sacrament, aware that in the conjugal pact there is expressed and realized the mystery that has its origin in God himself" (*AL* 213; see also John Paul II, Catechesis [June 27, 1984] 4, *Insegnamenti* VII, 1 [1984], 1941.

15. Marriage is not simply a contract; it is a graced "covenant" (*GS* 48; c. 1055 §1). Thus, the spouses are required, as Pope Francis puts it, to participate in a real "process of vocational discernment" (*AL* 72)—i.e., to establish a family that is truly a domestic church.

16. "One of their members is emotionally immature because he or she still bears the scars of earlier experiences. An unhappy childhood or adolescence can breed personal crises....Yet the fact is that only in their forties do some people achieve a maturity that should have come at the end of adolescence. Some love with the selfish, capricious and self-centered love of a child: an insatiable love that screams or cries when it fails to get what it wants. Others love with an adolescent love marked by hostility, bitter criticism and the need to blame others; caught up in their own emotions and fantasies, such persons expect others to fill their emptiness and to satisfy their every desire" (*AL* 239).

17. "The person with immature personality disorder adapts poorly to novel situations they find stressful. Their lack of emotional development also leaves them with a fairly fragile temperament and they are prone to quick shifts in mood. This is a person who finds great difficulty accepting responsibility for their actions and who will use immature defenses, such as blaming others, complaining

about ill health, or lashing out verbally or physically as ways to cope. Such defenses are quite common in children and often in adolescents but are viewed as highly undesirable in adults" (Jerry Kennard, "Spotlight on Immature Personality Disorder," May 6, 2012, Health Guide Info, http://www.healthguideinfo.com/other -mood-disorders/p113012/).

18. Many who "remain in the early stages of their affective and sexual life" (*Relatio Finalis 2014* 10) are simply not *capable* of committing to a unified life that addresses the marital problems sure to arrive. They are not fitted to the vocation of sacramental marriage. As was said at the 2014 synod, "Marital problems 'are often confronted in haste and without the courage to have patience and reflect, to make sacrifices and to forgive one another.'" *Amoris Laetitia* 41, quoting the Third Extraordinary General Assembly of the Synod of Bishops, *Message*, October 18, 2014.

19. "At times [new forms of communication] can foster apathy and disconnect from the real world. This 'technological disconnect' exposes them more easily to manipulation by those who would invade their private space with selfish interests" (*AL* 278).

20. In studying marriages, canon lawyers are often tempted to reduce "conjugal love" to the Scholastic concept of the will. They are to resist this normal temptation to settle for the abstract. Spouses must be capable of committing to an "affective love," a phrase reminiscent of the notion of *affectus maritalis* in Roman law and medieval theology (see *AL* 143).

21. "Tenderness...is a sign of love free of selfish possessiveness. It makes us approach a person with immense respect and a certain dread of causing them harm or taking away their freedom" (*AL* 127). Marriage requires that spouses contemplate each other as "ends in themselves," rather than as a means to an end (no. 128).

22. "Our teaching on marriage and the family cannot fail to be inspired and transformed by this message of love and tenderness; otherwise, it becomes nothing more than the defense of a dry and lifeless doctrine" (*AL* 59).

23. They are descriptions of divine love, of Christ, and of the spouses themselves. If one or both spouses are incapable of this kind of love; if they refuse to grant this kind of love; if they erroneously choose a relationship devoid of this kind of love; if they fraudulently deceive their spouse into thinking that they are

imbued with this generous love—their marital consent is invalid. There is no question that canon lawyers can use this analysis to develop a true Christian anthropology of marriage and, conversely, what truly amounts to "Christian pathology" that is destructive of the marriage bond.

24. The couple must not "view the wedding ceremony as the end of the road, but instead embark upon marriage as a lifelong calling based on a firm and realistic decision to face all trials and difficult moments together" (*AL* 211).

25. *Amoris Laetitia* uses Aquinas to point out this essential aspect of *caritas*: charity has no limits to its increase; as charity is exercised, the capacity for charity increases. "Nor on the part of the subject can its limit be fixed, because as charity grows, so too does its capacity for an even greater increase." *Summa theologiae* II–II, q. 24, art. 7.

7

The Newness of *Amoris Laetitia*

MERCY AND TRUTH, TRUTH AND MERCY

Julie Hanlon Rubio

On August 5, 2015, Pope Francis used his general audience to call for mercy for the divorced and remarried. "These persons are by no means excommunicated," he said. Though their "situation contradicts the Christian sacrament...it is important that they experience the church as a mother attentive to all, always disposed to listen in encounters."[1] The suggestion is that though those in second marriages are not formally excommunicated, exclusion from Eucharist makes them feel as if they were. His pleas for mercy and (implicitly) adaptation in pastoral practice became, to the surprise of many of the laity, the central point of debate during the Synod on the Family. Many who expected a clear decision in favor of mercy were disappointed both by the final document produced by the synod and *Amoris Laetitia* (hereafter *AL*), but so were many who wanted a clear affirmation of current Catholic teaching and pastoral practice.[2]

Catholic responses to *AL* diverge on the question of what Catholic laypeople need: truth or mercy. Some Catholic writers emphasize how new pastoral practices could contradict Catholic

61

teaching on marriage and be a source of scandal.[3] Others stress the healing brought to faithful Catholics by the pope's insistent refrain, "No closed doors. No closed doors!"[4] Some worry that the teaching on indissolubility is being eroded and point to the increasing acceptance of divorce that has led, first, to a steep increase in annulments and, second, to a significant decrease, as more Catholics divorce and remarry outside the church. Others who see brokenness in marriages they know are concerned, in contrast, that so far mercy has only inspired minor changes in liturgical practice, rather than greater moral acceptance of divorce itself, as more and more Catholics walk away from a church wedded to teachings that can seem untethered to reality.

Amoris Laetitia is more complex than these debates allow. The newness of *AL* for the laity—especially those in second marriages—lies not only in mercy but also in truth, in a strong vision of marriage as a deeply personal, lifelong, outward-facing union of two imperfect but committed people. The challenge of receiving *AL* will be discerning how mercy and truth fit together.

DIVORCE, REALITY, AND MERCY

For many Catholics who remarried without an annulment because they thought they could not receive one, the newness of *AL* lies in the possibility of inclusion brought about by changes in the annulment process. Already, a recent study shows increases in the number of annulment requests in many dioceses, after years of decreases.[5] Francis's annulment reforms may be especially important in immigrant parishes where the current annulment process presents particular difficulties (e.g., when spouses are in different countries, difficult to locate, in dioceses without tribunals or good records).[6] When the pope insists that "no one can be condemned forever" and offers a merciful path back to full inclusion in the church, many rejoice (*AL* 297).

However, many Catholics in second marriages do not feel annulment fits their situation. It seems unlikely that even eased procedures will lead a majority down that route.[7] In cases where no annulment is possible or desirable, *AL* seems to offer a second merciful path back: discernment of moral responsibility for the breakdown of their first marriage and readiness to return to the sacraments with the help of a pastor (see nos. 297–300). Some priests now feel empowered to reach out and open up new possibilities for people in their parishes. The advantages of this new path are real: respect for conscience, an invitation to adult faith, a recognition that, as theologian Margaret Farley has argued, because love is both emotion and will, it is fragile, which is both why we promise, and why we cannot make promises ultimate.[8] Many in second marriages welcome recognition of the reality of their finitude and affirmation of their fidelity to their new families.

The responsibilities of living into these new possibilities in second marriages are serious. Some argue against this path, for how can the reality of a first marriage be ignored? Because of God's grace, the ontological reality of a sacramental marriage never fully disappears.[9] In *AL*, Pope Francis encourages couples to consider whether a crisis in their marriage can become "an apprenticeship in growing closer together," while anticipating the need for parishes to accompany those who cannot stay together (nos. 232, 237). Perhaps part of accompanying people in second marriages will be helping them to ask hard questions: "How did I experience God joining me to my first spouse? Could God have been present in times of crisis? Where is God now in relation to us? Does anything of our marriage remain, even if significant parts have died? Am I experiencing God's grace and mercy in this second union? Is this where I am now called to be?" Receiving Pope Francis's teaching means balancing merciful recognition of human finitude and grace found in new paths with a willingness to look unflinchingly at what was lost and to mourn what was left behind.

MARRIAGE, IDEALS, AND TRUTH

But the newness of *AL* is not only in opening new paths but in giving a more compelling account of what marriage is at its core. Francis's move to speak directly to couples about their lives, especially in the fourth chapter of *AL*, is profound. John Paul II tried to do the same via his theology of the body and his four tasks of the family in *Familiaris Consortio*, but perhaps his philosophical and theological excellence limited his reach. Francis builds on this foundation and utilizes his pastoral skills to good effect, providing a vision that answers questions such as the following: "Why get married? Why promise to stay married for life? What does it actually mean to 'work on' marriage? What is the point of staying married if it is not making us happy?" Given declining marriage rates, and divorce rates that may be leveling off but are still high and even increasing among older couples, these questions need answering.[10]

Francis insists that deep, lifelong love is what human beings are made for. The promise to love another person forever "protects and shapes a shared commitment to deeper growth" (*AL* 123). Central to his vision is the goodness of love and intimacy, both of which need to be cultivated if marriage is to be sustained. Through inevitable disappointments, couples are called to embrace the joy of love, which can be experienced even amid sorrow (see no. 130). In marriage, two individuals become partners, companions on life's journey who promise to be there for each other forever, not just "until" (no. 163).

Embedded in this vision is a strong sense of the social nature of marriage. In marriage, love overflows, in children who should be raised to look beyond "self-absorption," but also in the social mission of the family (no. 276). Together, a married couple is "much more than two" (no. 181). They are called "to bind the wounds of the outcast, to foster a culture of encounter and to fight for justice" (no. 183). This is a vision of marriage that is worth signing up for and worth fighting for.

For married couples and those who are thinking about marriage or are afraid of it, *AL* can be a challenging source of reflection. Already, parishes around the country are transforming their marriage preparation programs to ready couples for the kind of marriage Francis speaks of, with longer programs, mentor couples, and a focus on accompaniment.[11] Possibilities for marriage renewal and education, which has been in decline in the United States, are just beginning to be explored.[12] With poignant, earthy descriptions of a married couple going deep, reaching out, and staying true to each other "even when," Francis offers a vision that can inspire and redirect.[13]

For couples living in second marriages, the vision of *AL* can be both inspiring and challenging. The vision could be inspiring for those in second marriages as they ponder, along with everyone else, how to become "more married," but challenging if a first marriage was left behind too quickly. In addition, it will be important to consider the complexity of second marriages. Certainly, many are life-giving for both spouses and children, creating new ties and obligations.[14] However, the social science data gives us a more sobering portrait: (1) they are usually entered into after periods of dating that involve instability for children, (2) they are more likely to end in divorce than first marriages, and (3) the outcomes for children do not differ significantly from those for children in single-parent families, which are troubling, even when finances are not an issue.[15] In short, those in second marriages will want to consider how their experience may reflect both the reality of love and grace so beautifully testified to in *AL* and the difficulties we know from social science.

Married couples considering divorce would benefit from placing the vision of *AL* for marriage alongside the social science data on divorce. There is some data suggesting that attempts to treat crises in marriage are inadequate. For instance, many marriage counselors do not have extensive training in couples counseling.[16] Most Catholic parishes lack capacities for supporting couples in crisis, and most couples do not seek help from their parishes.[17] Many couples do not receive support they need from friends and family. Focusing only on the mercy in *AL* may result in too narrow an emphasis on whether an exception to the rules applies.[18] Engaging the fuller picture allows for deeper questions: How serious is the suffering we are experiencing? How sure are we that our current suffering will continue? Do we have capacities beyond our imagining? Is growth possible or not? Who will suffer if we part? Even if we may divorce, should we?

Catholic communities charged with supporting the vision of *AL* have to ask, What social forces work against the forming and sustaining of marriages and what can we do to counteract those forces? How can we reshape expectations about marriage?[19] When divorce is a risk, can we help couples discern well? When divorce happens, can we carve out time and space to acknowledge both its tragic and healing aspects? Can we help those involved grieve and heal? Can we encourage better practices around divorce and postdivorce family relations? Through all of this, can we testify to our high value on marriage as well as to unfailing mercy for those who cannot stay true to the vows they made?

MERCY AND TRUTH IN PRACTICE

The newness of *AL* for the laity lies both in mercy and truth. For those in second marriages, I hope its push for more inclusion and more respect for moral discernment will open up new pathways back to the church. But I also hope that its rich vision of lifelong marriage inspires more struggling couples to continue keeping their vows, not out of fear, but out of hope and a desire for the kind of deep, generous, and enduring relationship Francis describes so well. And I hope that Catholic communities will be inspired to help couples: to better prepare for and deepen their marriages, to ask hard questions if contemplating divorce, and, if divorce and second marriage are the best option, to return to their parishes alongside the other sinning saints gathered around the eucharistic table.

NOTES

1. "Pope: Divorced and Remarried People Not Excommunicated," *Vatican Radio*, August 5, 2015, http://en.radiovaticana

.va/news/2015/08/05/pope_divorced_and_remarried_people_not
_excommunicated/1163121.

2. For a brief summation of reactions, see Mark Brum-
ley, "The Trending of the Pope," *Catholic World Report*, April
8, 2016, http://www.catholicworldreport.com/2016/04/08/the
-trending-of-the-pope/.

3. Ann Schneible, "Pope: 'By No Means Excommunicated,' but Divorce and Remarriage Contradicts the Sacrament,"
National Catholic Register, August 5, 2015, http://www.ncregister
.com/daily-news/pope-by-no-means-excommunicated-but-divorce
-and-remarriage-contradicts-the/.

4. Joshua J. McElwee, "Francis: Divorced and Remarried 'Are Not by Any Means Excommunicated,'" *National
Catholic Reporter*, August 5, 2015, http://ncronline.org/blogs/
ncr-today/francis-divorced-and-remarried-are-not-any-means
-excommunicated.

5. Dan Morris-Young, "Annulment Reform Seems to Cultivate Change of Culture," *National Catholic Reporter*, June 5,
2017, https://www.ncronline.org/news/people/annulment-reform
-seems-cultivate-change-culture. For the most up-to-date national
statistics on annulment, see CARA, "Frequently Requested Church
Statistics," assessed January 5, 2018, http://cara.georgetown.edu/
frequently-requested-church-statistics/.

6. Personal interview with Fr. John O'Brien, Our Lady of
Guadalupe Parish, Ferguson, MO. See also Brian Fraga, "Revised
Annulment Process Simplifies Petitions," *Our Sunday Visi-
tor*, October 26, 2016, https://www.osv.com/OSVNewsweekly/
Faith/Article/TabId/720/ArtMID/13628/ArticleID/20990/Revised
-annulment-process-simplifies-petitions.aspx.

7. Michael Lipka, "Relatively Few U.S. Catholics Skipped
Annulment Because of Cost or Complications," *Pew Research
Center*, September 9, 2015, http://www.pewresearch.org/fact
-tank/2015/09/09/relatively-few-u-s-catholics-skipped-annulment
-because-of-cost-or-complications/.

8. Margaret A. Farley, *Personal Commitments: Beginning,
Keeping, Changing*, rev. ed. (Maryknoll, NY: Orbis, 2013), 43–44.

9. Juan Jose Perez-Soba and Stephen Kampowski, *The Gospel of the Family: Going Beyond Cardinal Kasper's Proposal in the*

Debate on Marriage, Civil Re-marriage, and Communion in the Church (San Francisco: Ignatius, 2014), 86–87.

10. On marriage rates, see Wendy Wang and Kim Parker, "Record Share of Americans Have Never Married," *Pew Research Center*, September 24, 2014, http://www.pewsocialtrends.org/2014 /09/24/record-share-of-americans-have-never-married/; on divorce rates, see Scott Stanley, "What Is the Divorce Rate Anyway?" *Institute for Family Studies*, January 22, 2015, https://ifstudies .org/blog/what-is-the-divorce-rate-anyway-around-42-percent -one-scholar-believes; On "gray divorce," see Abby Ellin, "After Full Lives Together, More Older Couples Are Divorcing," *New York Times*, October 30, 2015, https://www.nytimes.com/2015/ 10/31/your-money/after-full-lives-together-more-older-couples -are-divorcing.html.

11. Peter Jesserer Smith, "A Year after '*Amoris Laetitia*': Marriage-Ministry Reform Sees First Fruits," May 25, 2017, *National Catholic Register*, http://www.ncregister.com/daily -news/a-year-after-amoris-laetitia-marriage-ministry-reform-sees -first-fruits.

12. Theodora Ooms, *The New Kid on the Block: What Is Marriage Education and Does It Work?* (Washington, DC: Center for Law and Social Policy, 2005).

13. Nicholas J. Healy Jr., "The Merciful Gift of Indissolubility and the Question of Pastoral Care for Civilly Divorced and Remarried Catholics," *Communio* 41 (Summer 2014): 306–28. See also Matthew Schmitz, "Anthropological Pessimism and Theological Hope," *First Things*, September 16, 2015, http://www.firstthings .com/web-exclusives/2015/09/anthropological-pessimism-and -theological-hope; and John Corbett et al., "Recent Proposals for the Pastoral Care of the Divorced and Remarried: A Theological Assessment," *Nova et Vetera* 12 (2014): 601–30.

14. Cardinal Walter Kasper, *The Gospel of the Family* (New York: Paulist Press, 2014), 45.

15. William J. Doherty and Leah Ward Sears, *Second Chances: A Proposal to Reduce Unnecessary Divorce* (New York: Institute for American Values, 2011), available at http://americanvalues .org/catalog/pdfs/second-chances.pdf. See also Andrew Cherlin, *The Marriage Go-Round: The State of Marriage and Family in America Today* (New York: Alfred A. Knopf, 2009).

16. Doherty and Sears, *Second Chances*. See also William J. Doherty, "How Therapists Harm Marriages and What We Can Do about It," *Journal of Couples & Relationship Therapy* 1 (2002): 1–17.

17. Elizabeth Marquardt, ed., *Does the Shape of Families Shape Faith: Calling the Churches to Confront the Impact of Family Change* (New York: Broadway Books, 2012).

18. This seems a danger in Kasper, *Gospel of the Family*.

19. John Paul II's high view of marriage may have been more harmful than helpful on this count. See Tom Hoopes, "Breaking Vows: When Faithful Catholics Divorce," *Crisis*, June 20, 2009, http://www.crisismagazine.com/2009/breaking-vows-when -faithful-catholics-divorce.

8

The Newness That Priests and People Face When They Receive *Amoris Laetitia*

AN OVERVIEW IN FRANCE

Msgr. Philippe Bordeyne

INTRODUCTION: A NEW PROCESS INVOLVING BISHOPS, PRIESTS, THEOLOGIANS, AND PEOPLE

*T*he commitment of the council "Family and Society" of the French Conference of Bishops has been remarkable, under the courageous leadership of Bishop Jean-Luc Brunin from Le Havre:[1] the objective was to have as many people as possible discover *Amoris Laetitia* (*AL*). This council prepared a commentary written by twenty theologians, male and female, belonging to a large spectrum of theological institutions.[2] The book also contains a guide dedicated to foster further reading and discussion in parishes. Around ten thousand books have been sold so far.

The background of this essay is my experience in the diocesan formations I have been invited to organize in twelve French dioceses, mostly at the bishop's initiative, often with the cooperation of the presbyteral council.[3] I have always been asked to focus on chapter 8, but I have each time started with an overview of the synod process led by Pope Francis, and of the theological impulse of *AL*, which can be summarized this way: the church is to serve God's action in the life of people who love and are faithful, always with their own limitations. In one diocese, the formation was addressed to representatives of parish councils, but usually it was reserved to priests, with the participation of deacons and laypeople in charge of the pastoral care of families. About one-half of the ninety-three dioceses of France have had such formations.

PEOPLE

People most often express the joy of discovering a papal document that is readable by nonspecialists, that deals with human sexuality, and tells of the beauty of love with ordinary words (especially chapters 4 and 5). Those who are more accustomed to theology notice the pope's call to avoid a discourse of the ideal disconnected from the concrete, and the call to respect the conscience of concrete persons who deal with concrete difficulties (see *AL* 36–37). They appreciate that the analogy between human marriage and the union of Christ with his church (Eph 5) is clearly designated as being always imperfect (see *AL* 122). They also note that a layperson, not only a priest, may be the right partner in the process of discernment in which the divorced and remarried persons are themselves to be actively involved (see no. 312).

Many married people express their joy and pride of discovering that Francis makes no taboo of aggressiveness, relational difficulties within the couple or between parents and children, domestic violence, marriage failure, divorce, divorced and remarried persons, or homosexuality. In France, there is a general feeling that more could have been said on unchosen celibacy, on people who deeply suffer from remaining single, and on couples who cannot have children.

However, I must confess that there is a gap between those who approve of the pope showing pastoral understanding toward family matters, and those who fear the pope might be fueling relativism by admitting that many people live in gray situations without being deprived of God's grace. In the second category, there are quite a number of young highly committed Catholics who expect from the pope a rhetoric of the ideal, rather than a realistic view on the real situation of families.

PRIESTS

A gap, similar to that among the laypeople, is noticeable among priests: some of them "have expected such pastoral change for years" (quotation of an older priest), especially the more inclusive approach to the divorced and remarried. Those priests appreciate not only pastoral mercy, but also a realistic approach toward human fragility, and toward the people we need to welcome or to keep within the church, especially parents who are the first actors for transmitting the faith. "Every family, despite its weakness, can become a light in the darkness of the world" (*AL* 66).

Conversely, other priests, especially the youngest, fear the lack of doctrinal safety in such a pastoral approach, even if they approve of a discourse on concrete family situations. Many of them have been raised in divorced families, or "patchwork" families, and they have entered priesthood with a high ideal (probably too high an ideal) of helping couples to reach stability and spiritual achievement in family life. One must also mention a small number of priests who, by principle, would never attend a formation on *AL*: they simply do not show up at diocesan formations.

In the two main groups, my feeling is that the reaction remains very emotional. The challenge is to have both groups enter into the text of *AL* beyond their own understandings of what family life and what pastoral of families should be. My experience is that a careful reading is facilitated when it is preceded by an engaged sharing of pastoral cases, avoiding starting with "difficult cases." It is preferable to start in a way that is congruent with the major theological impulse of *AL*: actively paying attention to the action of God's grace in people's lives, whatever their marital situation. In so doing, priests are challenged in their capacity for admiration rather than in their disappointment before fragility, or in their fear of betraying God's will. Conscience is capable and must be empowered: *conscientia capax, cum limites.*[4] Fragility requires our care for integration, but not our despair or our judgment. God knows our fragility better than we do, and he has saved the world through the death and resurrection of Christ. The mission of the church is to accompany this redeeming process, and to involve the recipients of salvation in the process rather than excluding them. The help of the church is owed to people who live in gray situations, otherwise the gracious action of God is despised. "By thinking that everything is black and white, we sometimes close off the way of grace and of growth, and discourage paths of sanctification which give glory to God" (*AL* 305).

MY INTERPRETATION OF THESE FACTS

In order to serve the reception of *AL* in the long run, I think it is necessary to clarify that Francis's change in moral reasoning is the clue to the change in sacramental discipline. The major resistance to *AL* probably comes from laity and priestly moral formation that is more doctrinal and intellectual, than pastoral and exposed to discernment in complexity. The same could be said about the formation in canon law, which should not forget the ancient tradition of judicial discernment.[5] I wonder whether and how case studies are being practiced in seminaries, regarding confession and spiritual direction. I suspect that priestly moral formation has been more focused on repeating the papal teaching of St. John Paul II, than on introducing varied moral traditions within the church history. Consequently, this makes it more difficult for priests to receive Francis's teaching as faithful to tradition, as long as it departs from an ethics of law, and revitalizes freedom and virtue ethics (see chapter 7 on moral education of the youth: education of freedom and formation of good habits). One should not forget that moral theology was born in the eighteenth century within the pastoral practice of confession (St. Alfonse Maria de Liguori) to facilitate the growth of people in the reception of God's grace on their way to salvation. And still in the first half of the twentieth century, continuous formation of priests trained them in pastoral discernment by discussing confession cases in local sessions under the authority of the dean. My experience is that priests suffer from being isolated in their pastoral discernment, which may increase their fear of being wrong or unfaithful. This requires places where every priest can speak freely and be respected in the views and questions he formulates. The contribution of laypeople who have experienced their consciences shedding light on complex situations would be helpful (see *AL* 37).

Learning to read a text is a real challenge, especially when it aims at practicing discernment instead of producing sharp judgments. For example, this is the question I was asked by a young priest at the very end of a session on chapter 8: "Why did the pope write the content of footnote 351 in a footnote and not in the main text?" The rules of interpretation certainly tell that the main text is more important than the footnote. Here, the main text says that the assistance of the church is required so that people can love and grow in God's grace when they are not "subjectively culpable" or "not fully," although they live in "an objective situation of sin" (no. 305). This means that the most important question to raise in the church is the following: How can we give assistance to sinners who are in a process of conversion and change (in other words, who are entering the state of grace) so that they can better cooperate with God's grace? This question is obviously faithful to the gospel and to Jesus's approach. Pope Francis denounces those who believe that some situations regarding law exonerate the church from giving her assistance. The question of sacramental assistance through penance and the Eucharist at the end of a serious process of discernment takes place in this larger framework. This is why Francis develops a deep theological discourse on the divine grace, and on the growing process it makes possible for people encountering various sorts of difficulties. This provokes the astonishment of many, as is the case in the gospel when Jesus let the sinners be part of the movement of renewal inaugurated by his preaching the kingdom of God.

NOTES

1. During the presynodal consultation, Bishop Brunin asked twenty-six theologians to write an answer to sixteen "difficult" questions. With the agreement of their authors, these answers were published, each question receiving several answers. The book opened the way to a public theological debate on marriage and family matters. (*Synode sur la vocation et la mission de la famille dans l'Église et dans le monde contemporain: 26 théologiens répondent*, Préface de Mgr Jean-Luc Brunin, Président du Conseil Famille et Société de la Conférence des Évêques de France, Paris, Bayard, 2015.)

2. Pope Francis et al., *La joie de l'amour—Amoris Laetitia: Édition annotée, avec guide de lecture et témoignages* (Paris: Éditions Jésuites, 2016), https://www.editionsjesuites.com/fr/livre-amoris-laetitia-la-joie-de-lamour-2034.html.

3. Out of this experience, I wrote a small book that also contains a text written by Juan Carlos Scannone, SJ, and Philippe Bordeyne: *Divorcés remariés: ce qui change avec François* (Paris: Salvator, 2017).

4. Philippe Bordeyne, "Conscience et discernement selon *Amoris Laetitia*: consentir à la grâce jusque dans nos limites," *Revue d'éthique et de théologie morale* 994 (June 2017): 91–104.

5. For example, the fact that the presence of an impediment arising from the divine law does not, in itself, delete the matrimonial consent. (Ludovic Danto, "Doctrine canonique et Exhortation apostolique post-synodale *Amoris laetitia*. Réflexion sur le consentement matrimonial et l'institution canonique des *sanatio in radice*: accompagner les familles en situation irrégulière," *Revue d'éthique et de théologie morale* 994 [June 2017]: 49–62).

Amoris Laetitia in Dialogue with the Secular, Disaffected (North Atlantic) Culture

9

Biography, Dialogue, and Evangelization

Cardinal Kevin Farrell

I want to offer a brief "thank you" for this invitation and for this consultation. This kind of meeting is very much in the spirit of Pope Francis's papacy and is explicitly expressed in the *Statutes of the New Dicastery for the Laity, Family and Life*. Therefore you, in effect, make my job easier! The text under discussion, I will argue, has deep roots in the pope's previous leadership in Latin America and characterizes much of his papal teaching. Allow me to start in Latin America.

BIOGRAPHY: ARGENTINA AND APARECIDA

The famous Latin American proverb "we all drink from our own wells" can be applied to the papacy of Pope Francis in at least two ways.

The first is that we can appreciate the papacies of John Paul II, Benedict XVI, and Francis as a triptych that respects their offering to the church wisdom from their own wells. Among other things, John Paul worked to describe and codify *what* the church teaches and lives (e.g., revised canon law, *Catechism of the Catholic Church, Compendium of the Social Doctrine of the Church)*; Benedict worked to describe *why* the church teaches and lives what it does (e.g., *Compendium of the Catechism of the Catholic Church)*; and Francis works tirelessly, in my opinion, as a living parable about *how* we should live what we believe, teach, and celebrate.

The second is that he continues to drink from the well provided by the wealth of pastoral life he lived in Latin America and as a member of the Latin American Episcopal Conference (CELAM). As archbishop of Buenos Aires, he saw the effects of poverty, unemployment, divorce, ecological devastation, and the intrusion of multinational corporations on a diverse population. In his initial foray into describing Pope Francis's papacy in the book *The Great Reformer: Francis and the Making of a Radical Pope*, Oxford professor Austin Ivereigh reminds us that this Jesuit pope regularly draws from the wellsprings of Ignatian spirituality.

As a Jesuit archbishop, Jorge Bergolio was influential on and the final editor of the text of the 2007 CELAM Aparecida document, which employed the "see, judge, act" method (no. 19). This extraordinarily rich text is titled *Disciples and Missionaries of Jesus Christ So That Our Peoples May Have Life in Him. "I am the Way, the Truth and the Life" (John 14:6)*. It deals with "the evangelizing action of the church" (no. 1) in a multifaceted text that touches on almost every aspect of Latin American church life and belief at the end of the previous decade, most of which is still applicable today. It should therefore come as no surprise that in addition to his pastoral experience, several key sections from the Aparecida document have become important themes for Pope Francis's papacy and writings. Its richness about evangelizing influenced *Evangelii Gaudium* (Aparecida, esp. nos. 28–379, understanding that this is the dominant motif of the whole document), its compelling arguments about ecology (in particular, ecological destruction) influenced *Laudato Si'* (nos. 24–27, 66, 83–97, 125–26, 471–75), and its powerful section on family life (esp. nos. 432–97) influenced Francis's desire to call two synods on the family (preceded by an unprecedented worldwide consultation) and to produce (with record speed) the postsynodal exhortation *Amoris Laetitia*.

DIALOGUE

In the Aparecida document, the CELAM bishops explicitly speak about the role of episcopal conferences and the communion between and among the churches. That a process of consultation and collaboration marked the final text of the Aparecida document is clear (prior to and at the nineteen-day meeting itself). That it has marked the papacy of Francis is clear from numberless references in his *corpus* to both *dialogue* and *encounter*. In the composition of *Laudato Si'* and *Amoris Laetitia*, the motifs of dialogue and encounter are equally clear, specifically in citing documents of episcopal conferences, previous popes (especially John Paul II's *Familiaris Consortio* and, among others, Benedict's *Deus Caritas Est*) as well as ancient and contemporary authors. In addition, in the case of *Amoris Laetitia*, the *Relatio Synodi 2014* was cited thirty-four times and the *Relatio Synodi 2015* was cited fifty-eight times.

In terms of the style and content of Pope Francis's teachings, the comment made at Aparecida by the CELAM bishops about church is very important, not to say central. The CELAM bishops asserted that "the gospel values must be communicated in a positive and forward-looking manner. Many say they are unhappy not so much with the content of church teaching, but with the way it is presented" (no. 497).

As many of you know better than I, last year Liturgical Press published the edited proceedings from a symposium held at Notre Dame titled *Polarization in the U.S. Catholic Church* (which includes a paper by our colleague Dr. Hosffman Ospino). By their nature papers from a symposium are not easy to summarize. But among the recurring motifs was one about church teaching and millennials. The authors regularly asserted that millennials do not want to be told what to think, to say, or to do. They want to be invited into dialogue and discussions, in that way feel respected, and make up their own minds. Here I will note two things: (1) the way teaching is presented and (2) characteristics of dialogue.

Regarding *the way teachings are presented*, for example, after discussing "the current reality of the family" (nos. 32–49), including extreme individualism, the fast pace of life, and fear of loneliness (nos. 32–35), *Amoris Laetitia* asserts that "we also need to be humble and realistic, acknowledging that at times the way we present our Christian beliefs and treat other people has helped contribute to today's problematic situation" (no. 36). The pope comments further on the "culture of the ephemeral," narcissism, fear of starting a family, pornography, prostitution, the influence of biotechnology on the birthrate, consumerism and the weakening of religious practice, lack of affordable housing and health care, migration, child prostitution, and so on (nos. 37–48), and then states,

> In such difficult situations of need, the Church must be particularly concerned to offer understanding, comfort and acceptance, rather than imposing straightaway a set of rules that only lead people to feel judged and abandoned by the very Mother called to show them God's mercy. (no. 49)

He then asks, "Who is making an effort to strengthen marriages, to help married couples overcome their problems, to assist them in the work of raising children and, in general, to encourage the stability of the marriage bond?" (no. 52). The word *joy* in the title *Amoris Laetitia* is coupled regularly in the document with words like "love and tenderness" (no. 59), which he argues should characterize our teaching, "otherwise it becomes nothing more than the defence of a dry and lifeless doctrine."

As a wise pastor, Pope Francis offers a number of recommendations about *how* to enter into dialogue (nos. 136–41), which "is essential for experiencing, expressing and fostering love in marriage and family life" (no. 136). They are the following: "take time, quality time" (no. 137), "develop the habit of giving real importance to the other person" (no. 138), "keep an open mind" (no. 139), "show affection and concern for the other person" (no. 140), and "for a worthwhile dialogue we have to have something to say....nourished by reading, personal reflection, prayer and openness to the world around us" (no. 141).

This is one area in particular where Pope Francis himself and *Amoris Laetitia* in particular can contribute to the contemporary culture of the United States. On the one hand, ours is a culture that has been characterized as partisan and polarized, bereft of heroes and ideals, where being consumed with the "self" triumphs over the communal. But on the other hand, our American culture is also one in which people help others in numberless charitable ways (e.g., recent grassroots relief efforts for hurricane victims) and where the term *first responders* is used to venerate all those who risk life and limb for others. To be faithful to the Catholic tradition in dialogue means that we need to have something to say and to stand for. Regarding marriage in our culture, this means standing for fidelity and permanent commitments in a "hookup" culture where smart phone apps offer opportunities for casual sex without commitments. Dialogue also means that we listen attentively to what the culture is saying about ways in which Catholic teaching has been distorted. It also means that we responsibly argue how Catholics are "believers *and* belongers," "spiritual *and* religious," respectful of all yet principled about the core of our beliefs.

One example of the way we might express our teaching would be to imitate the way the pope interprets 1 Corinthians 13 in *Amoris Laetitia* 90–119. This is really a commentary on daily life in marriage, highly insightful and easily accessible.

EVANGELIZATION

In *Laudato Si'*, Pope Francis asserts in several places that everything is interconnected and interrelated (e.g., nos. 16, 48,

49, 52, 56, 58). One of the major contributions of this encyclical is the pope's move from the "human ecology" of Benedict XVI to "integral ecology," specifically in chapter 4. Clearly, the word *integral* has been used repeatedly in the Catholic magisterium since Paul VI. It is a term that Pope Francis prefers as a way of synthesizing and consolidating church teaching and practice, as well as the way he has envisioned the recent changes in Vatican offices. The consolidation of the former Pontifical Council for Justice and Peace, Pastoral Care for Migrants and Itinerants, Pastoral Care Assistance for Health Care Workers, and *Cor Unum* to the Dicastery for Promoting Integral Human Development is a move in the direction of emphasizing "integral" development. The consolidation of the former Pontifical Councils for the Laity and for the Family into the dicastery I serve, "For the Laity, Family and Life," is another indication of emphasizing the integration of "life and laity" issues into one office.

But far beyond rearranging personnel and offices, what underlies these moves is Francis's vision that everything is interconnected and that, for example, evangelization is a central, integrating factor in his teachings and example. Put differently, this is to assert that the seeds sown in the Aparecida document, offering a wide-angle lens on a number of interrelated issues, have stayed with Francis in his papacy.

The specific paragraphs of *Amoris Laetitia* on "Proclaiming the Gospel of the Family Today" (specifically nos. 200–204) are part of the "act" section of the document that can only be understood by embracing the preceding arguments on "see" and "judge." These paragraphs are of a piece, interconnected with the rest of the document. The "gospel of the family" is intrinsic to Francis's vision for evangelization today. In line with the recommendations of the synod fathers in 2015, *Amoris* asserts that "enabling families to take up their role as active agents of the family apostolate calls for 'an effort at evangelization and catechesis inside the family'" (no. 200). This is immediately followed by the missionary challenge that this entails from the synod fathers' 2015 *Relatio*, which states, "This effort calls for missionary conversion by everyone in the Church… one that is not content to proclaim a merely theoretical message without connection to people's real problems" (*AL* 201). Who better to evangelize about the family than lay married couples, as well as couples who have had difficulties in marriage? Laity, family, and life are all intrinsically interconnected.

That the implementation of *Amoris* is a "work in progress" is attested by numerous initiatives, including the fact that Pope Francis has chosen "The Gospel of the Family: Joy for the World" as the theme for the 2018 World Day for Families in Dublin, whose program reflects and expands upon the chapters of *Amoris* itself.

We all drink from our own wells.

10

Amoris Laetitia and the Nones

Brian D. Robinette

THE RISE OF THE NONES

The question addressed by this essay is, "How will *Amoris Laetitia* assist the church's engagement with nones?" For those unfamiliar with this term, *nones* refers to those who when surveyed about their religious affiliation indicate "nothing in particular."[1] We might also use the terms *unaffiliated* or *disaffiliated* for our present purposes. As survey data show, a significant trend line appears in the rising number of unaffiliated persons in the 1990s, and in the latter half of the 2000s, we can observe a sudden, even startling uptick in their share of the U.S. population. To put a round number on it, whereas in 1987 approximately one in fourteen indicated "nothing in particular" when asked about their religious preference, today that number is one in five and inching closer toward one in four. This is an astounding development, given the historically high degree of religious affiliation in the United States, and it naturally raises the question as to whether the country is headed toward a "post-Christian" or "postreligious" future.

But there is considerable ambiguity in the data as well, for it turns out that the spiritual restlessness exhibited in the rise of the nones does not necessarily indicate an outright rejection of religious faith and its institutions, or that a growing "secularism," narrowly conceived, is afoot. Secularity is part of the story, but so too are new kinds of spiritual languages, narrative frames, and practices that are being born along the way, both within and beyond traditional religious frames.[2] I will return to this point momentarily, for my reading of *Amoris Laetitia* is that Pope Francis is making an appeal to family life that, while highly critical of individualism, presentism, and instrumentalist attitudes, is nevertheless drawing upon a language and set of sensibilities that are attuned to the spiritual restlessness of our age.

Although a comprehensive summary of the data on religious affiliation is not possible here, a few points are worth highlighting. Perhaps the most headline-grabbing data point in recent years comes from the 2012 report by the Pew Forum on Religion and Public Life, "'Nones' on the Rise: One-in-Five Adults Have No Religious Affiliation."[3] With an estimated 20 percent of the U.S. population declaring "no affiliation" with any religious group at the time of the report, religious observers, media outlets, and social commentators had a statistically round and eye-popping number to digest.[4] The number has only increased, in fact, and with an accelerated rate, according to the latest Pew study (2015).[5] The percentage of Americans who are now religiously unaffiliated ("atheist," "agnostic," or "nothing in particular") is closer to 23 percent of the population, which represents a 6 percent increase since a similar survey conducted in 2007. The percentage of American adults identifying as Christian is still considerable (seven out of every ten, making the United States the country with the greatest number of Christians in the world), but that number has decreased by nearly 8 percent of the population over the same seven-year period (from 78.4 percent in 2007 to 70.6 percent in 2014).

Christian denominations witnessing the greatest net declines are mainline Protestant and Catholic. In contrast to Evangelical and historically black churches, whose share in the population has remained relatively stable, mainline Protestants and Catholics have witnessed a noticeable decline over the past decade. Mainline Protestants now represent 14.7 percent of the population (down from 18.1 percent in 2007) while Catholics represent 20.1 percent (down from 23.9 percent in 2007), and together they account for 6.5 percent of the 7.8 percent total decrease in Christian affiliation. What sociologists call religious "switching" is one significant factor in these trends. Over one-third of Americans have switched affiliation from the religious tradition in which they were raised. Every group has therefore experienced net gains and losses, though some disproportionately. For example, whereas nones have increased the most on account of switching, Catholics have lost the most. For every person who switches to a Catholic affiliation, 6.5 persons become unaffiliated. This net loss to Catholic affiliation is nearly four times greater than it is for mainline Protestants. To put this in perspective, nearly one-third of American adults say they were raised Catholic. Around 41 percent of those no longer identify as Catholic, which means that 13 percent of all American adults are former Catholics. If counted as a denomination unto itself, the number of former Catholics would stand as the fourth largest in the country.[6]

Another significant factor in the rise of the nones is the generation-based change underway. Whereas 17 percent of baby boomers are unaffiliated, 23 percent of Generation Xers and 35 percent of millennials identify as "nothing in particular." This acceleration has led some to speculate that if current trends continue, the number of unaffiliated persons in the United States, together with those who identify with non-Christian religious traditions, will outnumber Christians within thirty years. Perhaps the United States is currently in a process of deep secularization, much like that found in Western Europe, where church attendance and religious affiliation have fallen precipitously in recent decades. Yet other observers are more cautious about such predictions. In their monumental study *American Grace: How Religion Divides and Unites Us* (2010), Robert Putnam and David Campbell express strong reservations about whether the rise of the nones implies that the secularization of Western Europe is paradigmatic for the United States. When we inquire further into the survey data to learn more about why the nones do not affiliate with religious institutions, or how in fact they do relate to them, if tentatively, a more complicated picture emerges. The nones, they insist, are not uniformly unbelievers; although less attached to religious institutions, they exhibit curiosity and inventiveness, if often eclecticism, with respect to religious beliefs, predilections, and practices. This is one reason why Putnam and Campbell have encouraged reference to "the somes" in the literature, or alternatively, "the liminals." These people "seem to stand at the edge of some religious tradition, unsure whether to identify with that tradition or not."[7]

What Putnam and Campbell also note, however, is that one of the major reasons for the increase in unaffiliation in recent decades has to do with ideological polarization. A significant degree of alienation from religion among younger cohorts has to do with backlash toward the alignment of its institutions and public figures with the political right, especially as this came to prominence in the 1980s. During the "evangelical boom" beginning in the 1970s and extending throughout the '80s and '90s, an increasingly articulate and mobilized form of Christian identity exerted considerable influence on conservative politics and achieved broad visibility in the public sphere. Premised on traditional values (or what has come to be called "family values"), the Christian right represents a particular sensitivity to shifting gender roles, sexual permissiveness, changing attitudes toward homosexuality, and strong opposition to the federal legalization of abortion. It is not surprising to learn, therefore, that as younger Americans were still forming religious attachments during the 1990s, many of them "translated that uneasiness into a rejection of religion entirely."[8] Neither should we be surprised that, as one Pew Forum survey puts it, "they became unaffiliated, at least in part, because they think of religious people as hypocritical, judgmental or insincere. Large numbers also say they became unaffiliated because they think that religious organizations focus too much on rules and not enough on spirituality."[9]

A DEEPER AUTHENTICITY

These are admonitions worth pondering, and I think it help-ful to see the content and tone of *Amoris Laetitia* as directly attuned to the restlessness they harbor. This is not to say that Pope Francis is uncritical of secularity and, more specifically, the strains of individualism, presentism, and instrumentalism that are quite dominant in contemporary society. The pope regularly criticizes "an extreme individualism," as he calls it, that dispar-ages institutions, weakens family bonds, turns freedom into caprice, and exhibits a fear of commitment (*AL* 33). He also calls out the dangers of a presentism that dismissively judges past gen-erations based on current tastes and norms, noting that derision of traditions and family structures cuts us off from a much-needed "historical memory" and a greater sense of filiation with our ancestors, with the elderly, and with the wider circle of fam-ily that situates us within a vast nexus of human relations (no. 193). And of instrumentalist attitudes Pope Francis is particu-larly critical, noting that affective relationships are not to be treated as material objects; that ours is too often the culture of the ephemeral that disposes of people when deemed no longer serviceable (no. 39); that marriage is too often regarded as a con-tractual agreement; that sexuality is poisoned by the mentality of "use and discard" (no. 153); and that children should never be the solution to personal needs (no. 170). In fact, Pope Francis's criticisms are so trenchant that one might suspect that he is essen-tially reactionary to the ideals and language of personal authen-ticity that come so naturally to younger generations, and that is quite evident among those who self-describe as "spiritual but not religious." But this is not so.

Taking my cue from the work of philosopher Charles Taylor, especially *The Ethics of Authenticity*, I see the tone and argumentative force of *Amoris Laetitia* as neither reactionary to the ideals of self-fulfillment in contemporary society nor supportive of them in their current form.[10] Pope Francis avoids blanket condemnations just as he avoids blanket affirmations. Instead, we find him affirming the moral force behind notions like self-fulfillment while challenging and deepening them. For example, after strongly criticizing a vapid individualism that makes an idol of autonomy, the pope immediately continues by offering a richer account of human freedom. "We rightly value a personalism," he writes,

> that opts for authenticity as opposed to mere conformity. While this can favour spontaneity and a better use of people's talents, if misdirected it can foster attitudes of constant suspicion, fear of commitment, self-centredness and arrogance. Freedom of choice makes it possible to plan our lives and to make the most of ourselves. Yet if this freedom lacks noble goals or personal discipline, it degenerates into an inability to give oneself generously to others. (*AL* 33)

The elements of this quote, I submit, provide a key for discerning the basic argumentative structure of the entire encyclical. What it does, in short, is (a) affirm the ideal of authenticity that appeals to so many persons today while (b) warning of its dangers and (c) challenging it and deepening it by connecting it to larger ideals, goals, and the work of discipline.

The way *Amoris Laetitia* does this most evidently is by appealing to the category of *growth*. Never do we see an attempt to browbeat the reader into submitting to an institution, and to this extent Pope Francis responds quite directly to contemporary suspicions of rules, codes, and rigid adherence to tradition. Instead we find appeals to personalism, to the cultivation of virtues, to the development of affectivity, to aspirations of wholeness. Life in the family, *Amoris Laetitia* argues, is a profounder, richer, more challenging way to realize human potential than offered by individualism—not, obviously, by making family the occasion for one's personal quest, but by undergoing a process of dedication, relationship, and growth through the joy and pain experienced with others. Genuine self-fulfillment is not condemned by the pope as mere egoism but affirmed as more truly possible in the context of committed relationships with others. The struggle here is not, therefore, over whether "authenticity" is a legitimate moral and spiritual source; rather, it's a struggle over defining its true dimensions and proper significance.

Speaking directly to younger cohorts—and here we can imagine him speaking specifically to the nones—Pope Francis writes,

> I would like to say to young people that none of [our deepest aspirations are] jeopardized when [our] love finds expression in marriage. Their union encounters in this institution the means to ensure that their love truly will endure and grow....As a social institution, marriage protects and shapes a shared commitment... to one another, for the good of society as a whole. That is why marriage is more than a fleeting fashion; it is of enduring importance. Its essence derives from our human nature and social character. It involves a series of obligations born of love itself, a love so serious and generous that it is ready to face any risk. (*AL* 131)

Notice here the direct appeal to young people, and notice also the category of growth operative in it. Our deepest aspirations are not negated by such an institution, but are in fact protected and made more meaningful by it. Marriage not only serves as an educative process for two persons who aspire to human fullness together, but it also contributes to the common good in all its interpersonal and social dimensions. It is not mere duty or convention; in other words, it is growth in authenticity.

To conclude, this is how I see *Amoris Laetitia* assisting the church's engagement with the nones. For those standing at the edges of religious institutions—the liminals, we might say—the encyclical serves as a public summons to embrace the personal and social goods of love in the family. While addressed to persons in the church, the encyclical's audience is much broader, and it expressly includes those who find themselves wary of traditional institutions, religious or otherwise. Of course, such engagement cannot presuppose that nones will pick up and read a papal encyclical as part of their own journey, but this is not how we should assess the potential effectiveness of *Amoris Laetitia*'s appeal. Rather, we should see in it the outline of an impassioned invitation, as well as an argument, that can assist those in the church who are called to witness to the wisdom of love in the family. It cannot be a requirement that this wisdom be lived only among the religiously affiliated, but the church has a distinctive role to play in publicly communicating and embodying that wisdom for the good of society, including when the religious character of that society is in a state of flux or even decline. Indeed, to the extent that a Christian way of life will attract those on the margins of religious belonging today, it will in no small part have to do with the way Christians embody love in the family as a path to growth.

NOTES

1. One of the earliest usages of the term can be found in Glenn M. Vernon, "The Religious 'Nones': A Neglected Category," *Journal for the Scientific Study of Religion* 7, no. 2 (1968): 219–29.

2. Some of the most illuminating studies in this regard include Nancy Tatom Ammerman, *Sacred Stories, Spiritual Tribes: Finding Religion in Everyday Life* (Oxford: Oxford University Press, 2014); Elizabeth Drescher, *Choosing Our Religion: The Spiritual Lives of America's Nones* (Oxford: Oxford University Press, 2016); Kaya Oakes, *The Nones Are Alright: A New Generation of Believers, Seekers, and Those in Between* (Maryknoll, NY: Orbis Books, 2015).

3. Pew Forum, "'Nones' on the Rise: One-in-Five Adults Have No Religious Affiliation," October 2012.

4. As Greg Smith, senior researcher for the Pew Forum, put it in a 2012 interview, the rise of the nones among millennials represents "a milestone in a long-term trend" (Cathy Lynn Grossman, "As Protestants Decline, Those with No Religion Gain," *USA Today*, October 9, 2012). See also Amy Sullivan, "The Rise of the Nones," *Time* magazine, March 12, 2012.

5. Pew Forum, "America's Changing Religious Landscape: Christians Decline Sharply as Share of Population; Unaffiliated and Other Faiths Continue to Grow," May 2015.

6. As the 2015 Pew Forum report puts it, "No other religious group in the survey has such a lopsided ratio of losses to gains" ("America's Changing Religious Landscape," 13).

7. Robert D. Putnam and David E. Campbell, *American Grace: How Religion Divides and Unites Us* (New York: Simon & Schuster, 2010), 591n56. The Pew Forum observes the same phenomenon, noting that "liminals" appear to "straddle the threshold of a religious tradition, partly in and partly out" ("The Rise of the Nones," 20n11).

8. Putnam and Campbell, *American Grace*, 130.

9. Pew Forum, "Faith in Flux: Changes in Religious Affiliation in the U.S.," April 2009, 8. Quoted in Putnam and Campbell, *American Grace*, 131.

10. Charles Taylor, *The Ethics of Authenticity* (Cambridge: Harvard University Press, 1991).

11

How Will *Amoris Laetitia* Assist the Church's Dialogue among Women?

Meghan J. Clark

*M*y topic for today feels impossibly big: How can this exhortation assist the church's dialogue among women within the context of secular, disaffected North American culture? As a Catholic woman, feminist, and moral theologian, my initial answer is: *it's complicated*. The very beginning of chapter 1, paragraph 9, begins with the title "You and Your Wife"—the text meditates on how male and female are together in the image and likeness of God; yet, the very frame raises the question, who is the audience? And so it's complicated. But I want to state with equal clarity that this document gives me much hope. I will focus on three points from *Amoris Laetitia* that I believe can assist the church's dialogue among women: an honest appreciation of feminism, an unqualified condemnation of violence against women, and a renewed support for the integrity of women's consciences and discernment.

FEMINISM

In an age of sound bites and social media, the diverse and multifaceted complexities of Catholic theology and of the many types of feminism are often reduced to intransigent debates about ordination, abortion, and contraception. On the ecclesiastical side, this often devolves into patronizing assertions of what "real women" want or need, with little space for the voices of actual women. When the fight for women's equality is caricatured in this way, feminism becomes the easy scapegoat of both conservative commentators and church leaders. Similarly, in this reduction, Catholicism is often caricatured by feminists and is then easily dismissed by many feminists as irredeemably patriarchal and sexist.

And so it was with excitement that I first read paragraph 54, in which Pope Francis unequivocally rejects blaming female emancipation for the social and cultural crises facing the family today. He states,

> The equal dignity of men and women makes us rejoice to see old forms of discrimination disappear, and within families there is a growing reciprocity. If certain forms of feminism have arisen which we consider inadequate, we must nonetheless see in the women's movement the working of the Spirit for a clearer recognition of the dignity and rights of women. (*AL* 54)

Catholic social teaching has long affirmed in principle and celebrated the growing recognition of women's equal dignity, but there is a shift in language and tone here that is significant. By specifically recognizing the *work of the Spirit*, theologian Megan McCabe notes that Francis "offers hope and belonging to many women who feel pain about belonging in the church, or who may have one foot out the door."[1]

In this important paragraph, Francis also points out the deeply rooted history of patriarchy and ways in which female exploitation and commodification continue today. Throughout the exhortation there are moments of insight in which Francis draws our attention to both the history and persisting reality of patriarchy and toxic masculinity. While upholding traditional church teaching, he says that "it is also true that masculinity and femininity are not rigid categories" and uses as a positive example rethinking traditional masculinity or fatherhood in our day (no. 286), which involves decoupling housework, childcare, and eldercare from femininity.

These provide fruit for dialogue among women in the church and for prayerful consideration by the church to increase women's participation and rhetoric in the public square.

VIOLENCE AGAINST WOMEN

Amoris Laetitia is a document addressed to the global church in all its diverse contexts. As such, there is a risk that we read its difficult passages as only being about *other places*. This is particularly a danger in the passages concerned with patriarchy and violence against women. In this document, Pope Francis emphatically condemns all forms of violence against women—naming domestic violence, female genital mutilation, as well as "lack of equal access to dignified work and roles of decision-making" (no. 54). Pope Francis goes so far as to state, "Every form of sexual submission must be clearly rejected" (no. 156) and targets specifically the ways certain interpretations of Ephesians or even 1 Corinthians have been used to subjugate women and urge them to tolerate violence. For example, Francis reiterates that *love is patient* "does not mean letting ourselves be constantly mistreated, tolerating physical aggression or letting people use us" (no. 92). In a particularly important passage toward the end, he recognizes that "in some cases, respect for one's own dignity and the good of the children requires not giving in to excessive demands," and that the need to prevent "a grave injustice, violence, or chronic ill-treatment" make separation not just "inevitable" but "morally necessary" (no. 241).

Attention to violence against women in this document is important pastorally and ethically. First, we must remember that, yes, Francis is addressing the United States. In 2017, there is not a single nation that does not have a problem addressing violence against women. According to the Centers for Disease Control and Prevention, one in three women in the United States will experience "contact sexual violence," and one in four will experience intimate partner violence in their lifetime.[2] Violence against women is not the exception, it is an epidemic—this should give us pause as we consider our congregations and classrooms.

Second, Francis does not sacrifice vulnerable women and children in his upholding of church teaching. This is one area where *Amoris* provides an opportunity for dialogue among women but also a challenge to the public witness of the church. In order for the document to assist the church's dialogue among women, we must allow our current priorities to be challenged by it. Violence against women is one place where the public voice of the church has not been particularly strong in recent years, even as sexual assault has been exposed as a continuing problem on college campuses, in the military, and in politics. In 2013, the USCCB withdrew its support for the reauthorization of the Violence against Women Act, despite previously supporting the bill. The USCCB cited provisions for lesbian and transgender victims of domestic violence as reasons to withdraw support.[3]

Pope Francis's unequivocal condemnation of the many forms of violence against women affecting the family and society is a crucial point from which to engage in deeper dialogue and action among women in the church. It also demonstrates perhaps the most persistent challenge of this papacy—to go to the margins and accompany the most vulnerable.

INTEGRITY OF WOMEN'S CONSCIENCES AND DISCERNMENT

A consistent theme throughout this seminar is the exhortation's attention to discernment and affirmation of conscience. In one of the most-quoted passages of *Amoris*, Francis states that the church is called "to form consciences, not to replace them" (no. 37), urging pastors and spiritual directors to "make room for the consciences of the faithful, who very often respond as best they can to the Gospel amid their limitations." Placing this toward the beginning of the text, Francis issues what moral theologian Emily Reimer-Barry calls an invitation to a grown-up faith and recognizes people's lives as *wonderfully complicated*.[4] Part of this is the challenge to assume goodwill and faith on the part of women discerning how to live out the gospel in their lives. The invitation to discernment found in this exhortation, as well as in *Evangelii Gaudium* and *Laudato Si'*, provides a strong point of departure from which we might deepen dialogue among women in the church. In particular, this invitation is likely to attract young women; insofar as *millennials* is a useful term, members of that cohort are often seeking integration in their lives—personal, professional, cultural, and social. They are attracted by integrated authenticity.

CONCLUSION

In preparation for this meeting, I asked some friends to look at *Amoris Laetitia* and share their initial reactions. I asked how they thought it might assist their own understanding of being Catholic women engaged in the church. In closing, I'll share two responses, both from married women who are practicing Catholics, neither of whom are theologians. One is a recently married woman in graduate school who found the document spiritually affirming of the complicated reality of marriage. The other has been married for over a decade, and has three children; her response was more challenging. She asked, "Where is the puke?" She spoke of the need to avoid romanticizing motherhood and marriage and to make more space for the messy and sometimes painful realities of life—for all the complexities of the persons in a family. To her, upholding the need to listen to and respect her conscience and discernment is paramount. And so I end where I began: How will *Amoris Laetitia* assist the church's dialogue among women? It's complicated, but there is much hope.

NOTES

1. Megan McCabe, "Pope Francis: We Must 'See in the Women's Movement the Working of the Spirit,'" *America*, April 8, 2016, https://www.americamagazine.org/issue/article/francis -family-and-feminism.

2. Center for Disease Control, "National Intimate Partner and Sexual Violence Data Infographic," updated April 28, 2017, https://www.cdc.gov/violenceprevention/nisvs/infographic.html. Full Report: "National Intimate Partner and Sexual Violence Survey 2010," November 2011, https://www.cdc.gov/violencepreven tion/pdf/nisvs_report2010-a.pdf.

3. "USCCB Committees Express Concerns over Domestic Violence Legislation," March 6, 2013, http://www.usccb.org/ news/2013/13-046.cfm.

4. Emily Reimer Barry, "Wonderfully Complicated: *Amoris Laetitia* as an Invitation to a Grown-Up Faith," Catholic Moral Theology Blog, April 15, 2016, https://catholicmoraltheology .com/wonderfully-complicated-amoris-laetitia-as-an-invitation-to -a-grown-up-faith/.

12

Amoris Laetitia and Hispanic Catholics

Hosffman Ospino

*I*n the English version of the 1981 apostolic exhortation *Familiaris Consortio*, the word *complex* and its cognates appear about four times.[1] Two of those times refer explicitly to the complexity of circumstances and realities defining family life.[2] In the English version of *Amoris Laetitia*, the word *complex* and its cognates appear seventeen times.[3] In fact, in the Spanish version, the word appears twenty times. The increasing recurrence of this term, even if it is merely a grammatical preference, reveals a growing awareness about the intricacies that go along with being family in our day. It calls all people of faith to acknowledge that the conversation about the family begins in the here and now of our lived reality: a reality that is complex and resists reduction to simplistic formulations or idealizations. The complex questions about marriage and family life today demand our undivided attention and common desire to work together for the sake of all families.

When we focus our attention on Hispanic families in the United States, there is no doubt that pastoral leaders, theologians, and educators must be attentive to the many complex realities that shape the lives of nearly half of all Catholics in this country.

We know that in the United States of America, about thirty-five million Hispanics self-identify as Catholic. They constitute about 43 to 45 percent of the entire Catholic population in our country. We also know that about 60 percent of all Catholics under the age of eighteen are Hispanic. About half of all millennial Catholics (i.e., young people approximately between the ages of eighteen and thirty-four) are Hispanic. The conversation about Hispanic Catholics is not about a forthcoming, possible future but rather about discerning how to respond effectively to a manifest present that demands that we grapple with it.

In what ways does *Amoris Laetitia* resonate and connect with the life of about half—the Hispanic half—of the Catholic population in the United States? To answer this question, I will refrain from merely commenting on specific sections of the document to draw lessons or venturing into some form of textual or conceptual analysis, both natural inclinations among theologians. Much of this has been done, particularly regarding the document's much-discussed chapter 8. While it is a very interesting and challenging chapter, there is a lot more to this beautiful document that also deserves our attention.

Keeping in mind the complexities of Hispanic family life in the United States, in this short reflection I highlight four opportunities that emerge from *Amoris Laetitia* to better accompany families within this sector of the U.S. Catholic population.

YOUNG HISPANIC FAMILIES: SEIZE THE MOMENT

The average age of Hispanics in the United States is twenty-eight. About half of all Hispanics in the country are younger than thirty. Two-thirds of Hispanics are younger than forty-five. When pastoral leaders and theologians in this country speak about family life among Hispanics, we cannot ignore that we are speaking about very young families with a large percentage of members who are children. Many passages in *Amoris Laetitia* directly address the daily relationships of parents, children, and youth in the sacredness of family life in the everyday. Pope Francis affirms, "If the parents are in some sense the foundations of the home, the children are like the 'living stones' of the family" (*AL* 14). Chapter 1 of the exhortation provides a beautiful meditation for Catholic parents and children to enter into the mystery of the family as a domestic church.

When speaking of Hispanic Catholics, it is important to know that although nearly twenty million Hispanics are immigrants, about thirty-six million more are U.S.-born. It is estimated that 48 percent of U.S.-born Hispanics are between the ages of eighteen and thirty-nine. These young people, along with Hispanic immigrants within the same age range, are at a point in their lives in which they are choosing careers and making important family decisions. As we can see, speaking of pastoral outreach to Hispanics in the United States is essentially speaking of ministry with Hispanic youth and young adults.

Amoris Laetitia is itself an invitation to turn our attention to the most urgent needs and the questions of young families. Here I think particularly of the young Hispanic Catholics who are transforming thousands of faith communities in the United States and redefining the entire U.S. Catholic experience. Thinking precisely about young families, Pope Francis asserts, "The synod fathers observed that 'the initial years of marriage are a vital and sensitive period during which couples become more aware of the challenges and meaning of married life. Consequently, pastoral accompaniment needs to go beyond the actual celebration of the sacrament'" (no. 223).

Advancing research on Hispanic Catholics in the United States grants me the privilege to engage in conversation regularly with groups of priests, deacons, vowed religious, and lay pastoral leaders. I often pose the following question: "How many of you in your parishes have established initiatives to accompany young Hispanic Catholic couples after they get married or start living together to raise children (a widespread practice)?" Normally one or two hands go up.

Most Catholic parishes in the country serving Hispanic Catholics do not have specific initiatives to accompany young families on a regular basis beyond what they offer during the Sunday liturgy and perhaps short catechetical moments prior to the reception of the sacraments. One good alternative to accompanying these young families should be Catholic schools, yet only 4 percent of Hispanic Catholic children are enrolled in these institutions.[4] Who is accompanying Hispanic families in these critical early years? We cannot claim naiveté, then, when we hear about high rates of divorce and separation among Hispanic Catholics—and Catholics from other cultural groups. Let us not forget that about 40 to 50 percent of marriages end in divorce in our country, most within the first years of the relationship.[5]

We need pastoral initiatives in parishes and instances of church life accompanying young families, particularly in the early years of marriage.

AFFIRM THE VALUE OF THE EXTENDED FAMILY

Amoris Laetitia makes a special invitation to affirm the important roles that relatives and others play in the life of the family. There is a pastoral obligation to accompany families in the complexity of their relationships. Many Hispanics live in family arrangements where grandparents, aunts, uncles, cousins, *padrinos*, *madrinas*, and close friends share the same space or live nearby. Often, many of these arrangements exist, particularly in the case of immigrants and families that experience high levels of poverty,[6] in order to ameliorate financial burdens and to make ends meet. Living as an immigrant or as a person earning low wages often demands that both parents spend most of their day outside the home working two or three jobs.

To illustrate this point, let us consider the following reality. About seven million grandparents in the United States live with their grandchildren. Forty percent of them (about 2.7 million) are responsible for all the basic needs of their grandchildren.[7] One-fifth of these grandparents live in poverty.[8] Hispanic and black grandparents, and the children they are raising, are over-represented in these statistics.

We must ask how the Catholic Church in the United States is accompanying Hispanic households with extended families as we affirm the value of marriage and family life. As observed, most Hispanics are Catholic. *Amoris Laetitia* offers this insight:

> The nuclear family needs to interact with the wider family made up of parents, aunts and uncles, cousins and even neighbours. This greater family may have members who require assistance, or at least companionship and affection, or consolation amid suffering. The individualism so prevalent today can lead to creating small nests of security, where others are perceived as bothersome or a threat. Such isolation, however, cannot offer greater peace or happiness; rather, it straitens the heart of a family and makes its life all the more narrow. (no. 187)

INTERGENERATIONAL AND INTERCULTURAL FAMILIES

Slightly less than one-third of Hispanic married adults in the United States (27 percent) live with a non-Hispanic spouse. While this is an increasingly common phenomenon that can generate great opportunities in a culturally diverse society like ours,[9] intercultural and interracial families experience unique challenges as well as tensions. Cultural and linguistic negotiations are regular aspects of life in these families. For Hispanic Catholics, how and under what circumstances the faith is practiced matters significantly (e.g., worship in English or in Spanish; choosing a faith community that is mostly Hispanic or one where being Hispanic is not highly regarded). Such decisions usually have an impact on how children form their Catholic identity.

In the context of Hispanic ministry, immigration questions play an important role in defining the everyday life and concerns of countless Hispanic Catholic families. As indicated earlier, about twenty million Hispanics are immigrants from Latin America and the Spanish-speaking Caribbean. About thirteen million of these immigrants self-identify as Catholic. According to the Immigrant Defense Project, "sixteen million people in the United States live in 'mixed-status' families, in which at least one family member is a noncitizen, whether a green card holder or an undocumented immigrant."[10]

Do Catholic pastoral leaders in the United States understand what rises to the top in terms of priorities for Hispanic Catholic families as they confront these situations? Do our Catholic faith communities, educational institutions, and ministerial organizations talk about these priorities with a sense of urgency? Do we understand the complexity of raising children amid these intercultural and intergenerational circumstances? Although sexual ethics and the pastoral care of couples living in "irregular" situations are important aspects of the church's pastoral and theological concern, our reflection so far invites into humble recognition the fact that the conversation about marriage and family life is much bigger, with added levels of complexity.

"In the replies given to the worldwide consultation," says *Amoris Laetitia*, "it became clear that ordained ministers often lack the training needed to deal with the complex problems currently facing families" (no. 202). Pastoral leaders, including many lay ecclesial ministers, often lack the intercultural competencies to accompany Hispanic families in their realities.

Of the nearly eleven million undocumented immigrants in the United States, about nine million are Hispanic.[11] Most of them are Roman Catholic. How do we in our dioceses and parishes accompany these Catholic sisters and brothers, their children, and the rest of their families? The threat and possibility of deportation is real for millions of Hispanic Catholics who are spouses, parents, and even minors. Deportation is a disruptive force in the life of many Hispanic families in our country:

> Graciela, a 51-year-old mother of four who declined to give her last name, made a plan to leave her two teenagers, ages 13 and 14, with her 24-year-old daughter, if she's forced to return to Mexico after living in Phoenix since 2004. "I want them to be able to finish their studies, but she won't be able to handle them for very long," says Graciela. "She has two kids of her own, and it's a lot to ask her. I've got to be prepared to take them back with me." Graciela is also devastated by the idea of leaving her older children behind. "I can't imagine not seeing my grandkids grow up," she says.[12]

Are we accompanying the Gracielas in our midst? How are we journeying with those women and men who live in fear because of the threat of deportation, those already deported, and the relatives left behind, especially the children?

Amoris Laetitia proposes that "while clearly stating the Church's teaching, pastors are to avoid judgements that do not take into account the complexity of various situations, and they are to be attentive, by necessity, to how people experience and endure distress because of their condition" (no. 79). To do this, it is imperative that the pastoral leaders studying in seminary, universities, and other ministerial programs are adequately prepared to discern, understand, and engage these realities. We need to cultivate with intentionality the necessary intercultural competencies to accompany Hispanic families and the families from all other cultural communities that constitute the church in this country. There is no alternative if we, as a church, want to remain relevant to our contemporary families.

THE NEED FOR STRONGER AND MORE WIDESPREAD ADULT CATECHESIS

A cursory look at the Catholic voices engaged in the conversation about *Amoris Laetitia* in the public square in the United States reveals that most are white Euro-American. Members of this group are constantly present in media outlets, Catholic and non-Catholic, speaking, writing, and debating about the insights and challenges of this apostolic exhortation. Most academics and experts writing about *Amoris Laetitia* are white Euro-American.

The prominence of white Euro-American Catholics in these public conversations correlates in many ways with their high levels of education. Approximately 55 percent of white adult Catholics are college educated. Most Catholic media outlets and most Catholic organizations and institutions in the United States are led by white Euro-American Catholics.

The proportion of Hispanic adults with college degrees is significantly low in comparison (18 percent). Most likely the majority of Hispanic Catholic adults will not participate in academic conversations about *Amoris Laetitia* or public debates in mainstream media outlets. Many of these Catholics are women and men doing their best to support their families with the little they have in the immediacy of their homes. Many have two or three jobs. This is not to say that Hispanic Catholics are not interested or have nothing to contribute to this important conversation. While the numbers of Hispanics engaged in the public square in conversations about the document may not be large, Hispanic Catholics are actively involved in conversations about marriage and family life. In fact, one of the strongest priorities that has emerged from the process of the Fifth National Encuentro of Hispanic/Latino Ministry[13] is precisely the family. Most Hispanic Catholics are engaging in this important conversation in small communities at the parish level and with their relatives. Hispanic mothers and grandmothers in particular play a major role in this conversation. This presents the Catholic Church in the United States with a unique opportunity for adult catechesis.

Yet the source of hope is at the same time a source of disquiet. While Catholic identity is strong among most Hispanics in the United States, one of the weaknesses of this population is the lack of solid adult catechesis. Although most Catholic parishes in the country serving Hispanic Catholics offer formal initiatives of adult catechesis, in English or Spanish, the number of Hispanic adults participating in them is miniscule.[14]

This is the appropriate time for Catholic dioceses and parishes serving Hispanics to launch adult catechesis initiatives with a clear focus on marriage and family life. The insights of *Amoris Laetitia* resonate strongly with many of the sensibilities of Hispanic Catholic families as they find their way in thousands of faith communities throughout the country. This must be an exercise of catechesis as empowerment. Yes, a catechesis that empowers Hispanic parents, children, spouses, and other relatives to discern and embrace their roles within the family, the church, and the larger society. A catechesis that empowers Hispanic families to encounter a living Christ. A catechesis that helps Catholics to grow in their faith. In this regard, *Amoris Laetitia* provides an excellent vision:

> The Church wishes, with humility and compassion, to reach out to families and "to help each family to discover the best way to overcome any obstacles it encounters." It is not enough to show generic concern for the family in pastoral planning. Enabling families to take up their role as active agents of the family apostolate calls for "an effort at evangelization and catechesis inside the family." (no. 200)

This will not happen automatically. Dioceses, parishes, universities, and other Catholic structures need to invest time and resources in Hispanic Catholics, especially the young. Demographics speak loudly and clearly. Hispanic families are playing a major role in defining the present and future of Catholicism in the United States. We must journey with them in the complexity of their experience.

NOTES

1. Pope John Paul II, *Familiaris Consortio*, nos. 15, 23, 31, and 66.

2. Ibid., nos. 15 and 31.

3. *Amoris Laetitia*, nos. 2, 32, 37, 41, 56, 79, 84, 113, 202, 206, 247, 249, 259, 287, 296, 303, and n344.

4. Cf. Hosffman Ospino and Patricia Weitzel-O'Neill, *Catholic Schools in an Increasingly Hispanic Church* (Huntington, IN: Our Sunday Visitor, 2016), 26.

5. See data and analysis from the American Psychological Association, accessed January 7, 2018, http://www.apa.org/topics/divorce/.

6. About 20 million Hispanics living in the United States are immigrants. Approximately 22 percent of Hispanics live below the poverty level. In 2015, the median income for Hispanic households in the United States was $45,148, nearly a third lower compared to that of non-Hispanic white households ($62,950), about 41 percent lower than that of Asian households ($77,166), yet about 18 percent higher than that of black households ($36,898). See Bernadette D. Proctor, Jessica L. Semega, and Melissa A. Kollar, *U.S. Census Bureau, Current Population Reports, P60-256(RV), Income and Poverty in the United States: 2015* (Washington, DC: U.S. Government Printing Office, 2016).

7. Approximately five million children live under these circumstances.

8. Alejandra Cancino, "More Grandparents Raising Their Grandchildren," *PBS News Hour*, February 16, 2016. Available online at http://www.pbs.org/newshour/rundown/more-grand parents-raising-their-grandchildren/.

9. See Gretchen Livingston and Anna Brown, "Intermarriage in the U.S. 50 Years after Loving v. Virginia," Pew Research

Center, May 18, 2017. Available at http://www.pewsocialtrends
.org/2017/05/18/intermarriage-in-the-u-s-50-years-after-loving-v
-virginia/.

10. See Immigrant Defense Project, "Impact on Families of
Mass Deportation," accessed January 7, 2018, https://www.immi
grantdefenseproject.org/issue-brief-impact-on-families-of-mass
-deportation/.

11. Cf. Robert Warren, "US Undocumented Population
Drops below 11 Million in 2014, with Continued Declines in the
Mexican Undocumented Population," *Journal on Migration and
Human Security* 4, no. 1 (2016): 9.

12. Sarah Elizabeth Richards, "How Fear of Deportation Puts
Stress on Families," *Atlantic*, March 22, 2017. Available online at
https://www.theatlantic.com/health/archive/2017/03/deportation
-stress/520008/.

13. See www.vencuentro.org.

14. In nearly half of parishes with Hispanic ministry, on average twenty or fewer Hispanic adults are reported to be involved
formally in faith formation programs beyond participation in
regular church services. See Hosffman Ospino, *Hispanic Ministry in Catholic Parishes: A Summary Report of Findings from the
National Study of Catholic Parishes with Hispanic Ministry* (Huntington, IN: Our Sunday Visitor, 2017), 36.

Amoris Laetitia Reaches Conclusions but, Even More, Opens Up Process

13

Discernment as the Landscape

NOTES ON THE ITALIAN RECEPTION OF *AMORIS LAETITIA*

Fr. Antonio Spadaro, SJ

I'm Italian. Many outsiders, especially Northern European and North American observers, enviously assess the Italian approach to personal morality as far more casual than that to which they are accustomed. It is an attitude of *lascia fare*, let it be, or, as the French would say, *laissez-faire*. There is some truth in this, but it is not the whole story. There is another deeply embedded current of moral rigorism that is also a part of the culture, which St. Alphonsus Liguori (1696–1787) addressed in his moral tractates. And elements of that rigorism remain. A great blessing of *Amoris Laetitia* is that it steers a course and gives a moral direction that is neither laxist nor rigorist. Its moral tone is evangelical realism.

Amoris Laetitia is perfectly tuned with what we read in the *Catechismo degli adulti*, by the Italian Bishops Conference, published in 1995, where we read, "Tending to the fullness of the Christian life does not mean doing what is more perfect in an abstract sense, but doing what is concretely possible."[1]

The key to understanding that evangelical realism in the context of moral choices is discernment. I want now to explore in some detail the process of discernment that *Amoris Laetitia* opens up considering the Italian context and approach.

DISCERNMENT GOES BEYOND ABSTRACTIONS

Discernment refers directly to the conscience and to historicity. The Italian way of thinking, the Italian philosophy since Giovanni Battista Vico (1668–1744)—Neapolitan like Liguori—for example, is grounded in history. Vico inaugurated the modern field of the philosophy of history. For Vico, by looking at particular facts of history, at historical evidence, it is possible to understand better the truth and even to make metaphysical claims. This is, basically, the Italian way of thinking.

And, of course, now it is clear why the message of Pope Francis resonates in our souls and minds. Pope Francis often repeats that one danger that must be avoided—and a danger to which in fact one often succumbs—is being abstract, theoretical, and idealistic. He writes, "This excessive idealization, especially when we have failed to inspire trust in God's grace, has not helped to make marriage more desirable and attractive, but quite the opposite" (*AL* 36).

It would be an illusion to believe that people are given assurance and consolation in their values solely because we insist on preaching doctrine without adequately "*mak[ing] room for the consciences* of the faithful, who very often respond *as best they can* to the Gospel amid their limitations, and are capable of carrying out their own *discernment* in complex situations. We have been called *to form consciences, not to replace them*" (no. 37, my italics).

It is important to insist on "a positive and welcoming

pastoral approach capable of helping couples to *grow* in appreciation of the demands of the gospel" (no. 38, my italics). Growth implies time, history. With regard to wounded situations and to those that are called "irregular," the exhortation takes over from the *Relatio Finalis* of the ordinary synod, the complex criterion that St. John Paul II formulated in *Familiaris Consortio*: the "careful discernment of situations" (no. 84). The exhortation takes over from the synod the itinerary of discernment in individual cases, without placing limits on integration (as was done in the past). It also states that it is undeniable that under some historical circumstances, "imputability and responsibility for an action can be diminished or even nullified" (*AL* 302)[2] by various factors. "For this reason, a negative judgment about an objective situation does not imply a judgment about the imputability or culpability of the person involved" (no. 302).

We must conclude that the pope realizes that one can no longer speak of an abstract category of persons, enclosing the praxis of integration in a rule that is absolutely general and valid in every instance. "Since 'the degree of responsibility is not equal in all cases,' the consequences or effects of a rule need not necessarily always be the same" (*AL* 300).

So Pope Francis affirms that *"it can no longer simply be said that all those in any 'irregular' situation are living in a state of mortal sin and are deprived of sanctifying grace"* (no. 301, my italics). It's not just a matter of ignorance of the rule. A subject may know the rule well, but have great difficulty in understanding its inherent values. A person could even live in a concrete situation that does not allow him or her to act differently and decide otherwise without further sin. Factors may exist that limit the ability to make a decision. Conscience can also recognize with sincerity and honesty what for now is the most generous response that can be given to God.

It follows that "in an objective situation of sin—which may not be subjectively culpable, or not fully such—a person can be living in God's grace, can love and also grow in the life of grace and charity, while receiving the Church's help to this end" (no. 305).

TOWARD A PASTORAL CONVERSION

This is why discernment is so crucial. It's a constant process of opening oneself to the word of God, so that it can shed light on the concrete reality of every life. This process leads us to be docile to the Spirit, who encourages each one of us to act with love, in the concrete situation and within the bounds of what is possible, and who moves us to grow from the good to the better. So the synod had declared that "priests have the duty to 'accompany [the divorced and remarried] in helping them to understand their situation according to the teaching of the Church and the guidelines of the bishop'" (no. 300).

The bishops of the different churches in the world are giving guidelines. The Italian church, like all the churches of the world, has noted reasons for enthusiasm, but also resistance made more or less explicit. Considering Italy, the clearest explication of the perspective of *Amoris Laetitia* comes from the regional Bishops Conference of Sicily. In a document of June 4, 2017, "pastoral guidelines" were expressed that articulate three stages according to the chapter 8: accompanying, discerning, integrating.[3]

Discernment is central. We read, "The formulations of *AL* open cautiously to an eventuality of access to the sacraments, that is situated only in the dialogic place of discernment: it is not a canonical norm, but the potential of a path, fruit of discernment and personal and pastoral maturation, exists (cfr *AL* 298)" (no. 1).

The effort of integration has its fulcrum in the *practice* of discernment. It is distinguished into pastoral and personal:

Pastoral discernment: indicates the task of pastors, first of all bishop and priests, when confronting people or situations that are the object of pastoral action. It aims to grasp the particularity of the differences and

118

of the various situations, taking into consideration the set of circumstances—subjective and objective—putting them into relationship with the teaching of the Church and of the bishop (cfr *AL* 300), showing the faithful the paths of faithfulness and growth of Christian life in the situations considered. (2.2.1)

Personal discernment: indicates, instead, specifically the discernment exercised in the first person of the faithful, when faced with the need to make a decision in order to act in a particular situation. To live as a Christian, it is supposed that whoever acts seeks to be faithful to the will of the Lord, which is manifested in the situation itself. Moreover, it is why the faithful turns to the pastor. (2.2.2)

On discernment, it clearly states, "It is the principal task of priests to accompany people involved on the path of discernment, according to the teaching of the church and the guidelines of the bishop" (2.2). Discernment, according to the Sicilian bishops, "allows pastors to evaluate case by case, especially regarding the progressive inclusion of people who, finding themselves in a situation by now irreversible, are particularly in need of welcome, accompaniment and mercy" (2.3).

The Sicilian document concludes with clarity that "in some circumstances, therefore, regarding the divorced and remarried, according to the evaluation of the confessor and taking into account the good of the penitent, it is possible to grant absolution and to admit him or her to the Eucharist, even if the confessor knows that it is an objective disorder for the church" (2.2.4c).

Then it is no longer possible to judge people based on a norm that stands above everyone's heads and ignores real life. The pastor must involve himself in the life of the person in front of him. And our formation is not always up for this challenge. In Italy this challenge, which involves seminarians, the theology faculty, and the formators, is recognized.

In a private talk with the Polish Jesuits during his trip to World Youth Day in 2017, Pope Francis said that sometimes the priestly formation programs

> run the risk of educating in the light of overly clear and distinct ideas, and therefore to act within limits and criteria that are rigidly defined a priori, and that set aside concrete situations: "you must do this, you must not do this." And then the seminarians, when they become priests, find themselves in difficulty in accompanying the life of so many people and adults.[4]

What the Sicilian document clearly is aware of is the significant difficulty that *Amoris Laetitia* poses for some pastors who insist on dealing exclusively with the binary division of "state of grace" and "state of sin." Of course, there is a state of grace and a state of sin, because we can be in a loving relationship with God. And that means his indwelling or sanctifying grace. Alternately, we can be in a state of sin or alienation from God. For example, I may be in the state of grace and negligent in such a way that the quality of that relationship is eroding and may even become susceptible to rupture. I may be in the state of sin and continue the downward spiral of alienation. But I may be in the state of sin with nudges of actual grace that little by little push me toward repentance and a conversion of heart. An emphasis on the "state" of a person or family or marriage, however, situates people, by definition, in a static position. We Italians have a historical way of thinking.

This is why in recent years Pope Francis has worked at length to renew the Italian Bishops Conference, given the high number of pastors who have reached seventy-five years of age. This year there was also the turnover of the president of the conference. The pope's recent nominations have had a strong pastoral character. The vicar of Rome and the archbishop of Milan are both formators of the clergy, very beloved by their priests, who worked for some time along these lines. Also, some cardinal nominations have made still more evident pastorality as a central criterion.

NOTES

1. Conferenza Episcopale Italiana, *La verità vi farà liberi. Catechsimo degli adulti* (Vatican City: Libreria Editrice Vaticana, 1995), 919.

2. Also see *Catechism of the Catholic Church* 1725.

3. Conferenza Episcopale Siciliana, *Orientamenti pastorali. Accompagnare, discernere, integrare la fede secondo le indicazioni del cap. VIII di Amoris laetitia*, at http://www.chiesedisicilia .org/cesi/allegati/5928/Orientamenti%20Pastorali%20Amoris %20Laetitia%20def.pdf, accessed January 7, 2018.

4. Papa Francesco, "Oggi la Chiesa ha bisogno di crescere nel discernernimento. Un incontro privato con alcuni gesuiti polacchi," *La Civiltà Cattolica* 3 (2016): 345–49, at 348.

14

Diocesan Topical Synods

A PATHWAY FOR PASTORAL CONSULTATION IN THE LOCAL CHURCH

Bishop Robert W. McElroy

The issuance of *Amoris Laetitia* provided us in the Diocese of San Diego with an opportunity to examine whether a pattern of regular diocesan synods on specific topics could constitute an effective, collaborative, and faith-filled avenue for sustainable pastoral reflection and planning. The apostolic exhortation addressed a pivotal facet of the life of the gospel in the contemporary world, its topic represented an issue area in which lay insights have particular depth and authority, and the results of a synodal process could reach into all levels of life in the local church precisely because marriage and family life suffuse both the human experience and the ecclesial experience in every dimension.

For these reasons, in early 2016, the diocesan pastoral curia of San Diego began to investigate the idea of holding a diocesan synod to promote the reception and application of Pope Francis's exhortation to the church on marriage and family life.

There were several obstacles to undertaking such a journey. The first was ascertaining whether it was possible in church law to have a diocesan synod on one specific topic. After hearing from a variety of canonist friends, a rather uniform response of "Well, I have never heard of one, but I don't know of any legal provision that precludes it," our planning team concluded that that was permission enough, and we pressed on.

The second obstacle surfaced in the initial consultations with the presbyteral council and the lay leadership of the diocese. They were, in general, open to and even intrigued by such a project, but they pointed to one central imperative: the synod must result in conclusions that could be implemented, and there had to be sustained follow through. Several of the senior priests and lay leaders recalled that the last diocesan synod several decades before had not witnessed substantive implementation, leaving everyone deflated.

The third obstacle was the most daunting. The priestly and lay leadership pointed out that if this synodal process was to be a recurring pathway of consultation and implementation, it was essential that the process be contoured in advance to a timeline of no more than two years in total for the planning, the work of the preparatory committees, the holding of the synod itself, and substantive implementation. Thus, at every step in the design process, it was essential to hew to a fairly strict timeline, a requirement that at times demanded sacrificing some elements of breadth and depth in consultation and inclusion.

Paulist Fr. John Hurley, the former staff director for evangelization at the USCCB, agreed to plot out and oversee the process. The subject matter for the synod was drawn from *Amoris Laetitia* and focused on five issue areas: witnessing to the beauty and richness of the Catholic vision of marriage; forging a culture of invitation within our parishes to young couples; nurturing children; spirituality in family life; and ministry to those who have been divorced.

The 142 delegates included the presbyteral council, one lay delegate from each of the ninety-nine parishes of the diocese, four deacons, and five women religious, as well as representatives from the young-adult communities in our colleges and universities. The parish representatives were appointed by their pastors, and happily their median age was only forty-one. The delegates manifestly represented the great ethnic and cultural diversity of our local church.

In the months before the synod, delegates were assigned to their choice of five working committees, one for each of the five topics from *Amoris*. In addition, we assigned a different theologian to each of the working groups, a decision that was really undertaken just because we thought there should be theologians in a synod, but in fact it was a decision that would enrich substantially the work of the synod. Each of the parish representatives held listening sessions in their parishes on the specific topic of their committees, and the results were collated and distributed to every member of the relevant working committee.

The synod itself was a weekend gathering devoted to prayer and reflection on the specific pastoral proposals developed by the working groups in order to refine them and then adopt those that seemed most pressing and attainable. The overarching theme of the gathering spoke to this emphasis on prayer, reflection, and unity: "We recognize that this very act of gathering in the name and grace of our God is a profound declaration of ecclesial identity, hope, and witness." There was in fact a wonderful sense of hope and witness throughout the gathering, and fifteen proposals emerged for pastoral action. Even in moments of debate over the direction of specific proposals, there was a palpable sense of God's guiding and joyful presence.

For me as a bishop, both the beauty of the weekend experience and the quality of the proposals that emerged were very powerful. But for the purposes of this gathering, five aspects of the synod process were particularly illuminating:

1. There was a burning desire to provide an intensely welcoming stance to young couples as they approach the church on questions of marriage and family life. Overwhelmingly, the delegates believed that the

church is in a moment of crisis in its relationship with the millennial generation and that this necessitates an unwavering strategy of outreach and welcome. We must take young couples where they are and walk with them toward marriage, but not balk or nag when their progress is too slow. The delegates also shared horror stories from young adults they knew who had experienced the church and the parish as presenting to them not a welcome mat, but an ever-expanding set of hoops they must jump through in order to get married.

2. The working groups and synod gathering itself displayed a continual commitment to inculturation in applying the teachings of *Amoris* and the church to the concrete realities of the church in San Diego. One long discussion at the working group on nurturing children illustrates this focus. The committee was discussing the need to reach out in a special way to single-parent families. As they talked, they came to the conclusion that this outreach must look different in San Diego because of our social reality. For most of the United States, single-parent families are those in which death or divorce has severed a marriage or in which there was no marriage to begin with. San Diego, the committee said, includes these three realities, but it also includes two other groups: the deployed and the deported. San Diego's immense military population and the number of families broken by our national immigration policy mean that our outreach to single families must look and operate in a different manner. This process of applying church teaching based on the specific realities of a particular diocese suffused the entire synodal process of formulating proposals for action, and it constitutes, I think, one of the central benefits of a synodal process.

3. As the process of the synod unfolded, the focus on family spirituality grew more intense. There was a great perception and fear that families, especially young families, do not have a spiritual dimension to their marriages or their relationship with their children. They cannot teach their children affectively about God because their marriages have no place for prayer and spiritual realities. The synod ultimately concluded that the diocese's outreach program for marriage and family should be called the Office of Family Life and Spirituality to point to the need to place spirituality at the heart of every step of implementing *Amoris* and the synod.

4. The discussions on the questions posed in chapter 8 took on a trajectory that our planning committee had not foreseen. There was very broad support for widening the pathway to Eucharist for the divorced and remarried; more than four-fifths of the delegates sought a teaching even broader than *Amoris*, and they felt that this question raises substantive issues about the compassion of the church. But beyond this, the longest and most profound discussions of chapter 8 touched on the core doctrine of conscience. When the delegates encountered the richness of our Catholic approach to conscience formation and decision-making during the theological presentations of the San Diego synod, they protested that they had never heard this before and felt as though a critical part of their faith had not been communicated to them, with the result that their moral decision-making and peace of mind had been hobbled throughout their lives. It must be emphasized that the delegates' enthusiasm for the rich tradition of conscience did not spring from any perception that conscience is a get-out-of-jail-free card, but from a conviction that the Catholic doctrine on conscience takes seriously

the daunting dilemmas, the mixed motivations, the paralyzing personal issues, and the doubts that characterize adult moral life. The delegates made one of their most emphatic conclusions the need for a wide-ranging program of education about conscience and moral decision-making at all age levels.

5. The fifth aspect of our synodal process that struck me as important has to do with something Pope Francis often emphasizes: the importance of encounter. While synod participants came to find broad agreement about widening a path to the Eucharist for the divorced and remarried, not everyone arrived at the synod sharing the same opinions. Indeed, some of the conversations featured significant disagreements. But in the give-and-take of honest dialogue, what broke through these barriers was something deceptively simple, yet crucial to any synodal process: the sharing of our stories. So often, questions of norms—ecclesial or otherwise—operate on the level of the abstract. From that vantage point, deciding what is on the right or wrong side of whatever rule is up for discussion can seem almost easy. But when synod delegates brought their own narratives to the conversation, barriers broke down and the concrete situations of our people began to influence the ways in which we considered these pastoral challenges.

After the synod concluded, it was essential to move quickly toward implementation. The planning team caucused and identified twenty-three names of delegates who should be approached to serve on a fifteen-month implementation committee. All twenty-three agreed to serve.

They adopted a two-pronged strategy: redesigning the entire process of marriage preparation to follow a more catechumenal model and using pilot parishes to create models for integrating the principles of *Amoris* into the diocese. Twelve pilot parishes stepped forward to radically recast their approach to marriage ministry by applying the fifteen mandates of the synod in their ecclesial life. Each parish formed a marriage and family leadership team of volunteer couples and single parishioners who committed themselves to the implementation effort so that the pastor and parish staff would not be overly burdened. Like many elements of the synod, implementation in the pilot parishes took a much different pathway than we had anticipated. Originally, we were looking for a common parish model to emerge for diocesan-wide implementation. But because the pilot parishes varied dramatically in their makeup, the initiatives they adopted in furtherance of the synod principles were extremely diverse. Immigrant parishes emphasized base group initiatives for married couples. Anglo parishes with large numbers of young couples focused on supportive structures for nurturing community, enduring crises, and beginning spiritual growth within the family. We have many parishes with relatively few young couples, and these have created strategies focused on long-term marriages, the stresses of age in marriage, and the need to celebrate the success of married life. Each of these pilots is the story of a parish attempting strenuously to embrace the synodal propositions. But the pathways of implementation have been wildly different and creative.

One vital element of the integration of the synodal process into the life of the church took place during a recent annual weeklong convocation of priests. The week was dedicated to the principles of *Amoris*. Father Louis J. Cameli spoke about the formational identity of the document and the role of conscience. Our new marriage and family life office staff presented the catechumenal model of marriage preparation, and I dialogued with the priests about chapter 8 and the internal forum. There was significant enthusiasm and openness, and some reservations. Overall, the widespread sense among the priests that we are in a state of crisis regarding marriage and young adults generated wide support for moving forward.

How successful was the synodal process in San Diego? It produced focused, prayerful, broadly based reflections on the central issues presented by *Amoris Laetitia* in our local church. It called forth a series of creative new initiatives that are realistic and capable of being implemented. It was a moment of revelation that brought through lay experience and witnessed a greater recognition of the specific ways in which the church itself creates obstacles for young couples seeking marriage, the divorced, single parents in distress, and members of the LGBT communities. It was short enough and limited in its aspirations so that it did not produce exhaustion.

At the same time, this synodal model has definite limitations. A topical synod cannot explore the wide linkages among ecclesial issues that a general synod can. The short timeline for designing the synod did not allow the depth of parish-based consultation that would have enriched the process and engaged more members of the diocese in it. The consensus-based approach tended to underplay the significant divergences among delegates, and thus San Diego Catholics, about neuralgic issues.

In summary, the process of a topical synod is a powerful tool for expansive pastoral planning in a diocese on one wide segment of ecclesial life. It teaches bishops much about how laymen and -women wrestle with the issues that we write and speak and teach about. And it is a moment for the palpable presence of God to touch a local church.

15

Does Synodality Help
the Church Live Out Her
Mission Today?

Richard R. Gaillardetz

Our conference has been reflecting on the significance of *Amoris Laetitia* for the work of moral formation and pastoral practice. This session invites reflection on questions of ecclesial process. If we attend to the ecclesial processes associated with *Amoris Laetitia*, our attention can move in two directions: first, toward the ecclesial processes and presuppositions that gave rise to this remarkable document, and second, toward the present ecclesial moment in which the document is being received. Considering the first, we can note the remarkable preparation and conduct of the two synodal assemblies: the unprecedented processes for consulting the faithful, the inclusion of the testimony of married couples, and the remarkable papal encouragement to *parrhesia*, candid speech.

When we consider the ecclesial reception of the document, the first thing to note is the papal encouragement of *Amoris Laetitia*'s regional implementation. Let's be clear about what is going on here: what the pope has been encouraging is nothing less than an ecclesial application of the principle of subsidiarity, the very application that had been forcefully rejected but a few decades earlier. We must also acknowledge the open debate surrounding the document. That debate has certainly included wide-ranging appreciations like those that have dominated our own conversation. But there have also been instances of harsh criticism, including the publication of *dubia* and "filial corrections" of Francis, which publicly raised concerns about how *Amoris* treats the issue of communion for the divorced and remarried, even as these instruments have relied on historically and pastorally decontextualized renderings of doctrinal propositions. Indeed, a striking feature of our contemporary moment is that few expect there to be any ecclesiastical censure for either the authors of the *dubia* or the signatories of the most recent "filial correction" of Pope Francis. Our church is currently being led by a pastor who is remarkably undisturbed by accusation. But this forbearance is not just a papal personality trait. In my view, Francis has not responded to these attacks because he does not accept the presupposition that authority works exclusively along a vertical axis. The very language of "filial" correction, emphasizing a parent–child exercise of authority, presumes that ordinarily authority is exercised in an exclusively descending direction. Only in the most extraordinary of circumstances, papal heresy, for example, is the movement on that axis reversed. Francis, by contrast, imagines a more pluriform and multidirectional exercise of authority, in which genuine authority—or more accurately, authorities—contributes to the whole church as its members learn to listen to others, including those with whom they disagree.

If we draw back our gaze from focused consideration of the preparation for, and reception of, *Amoris Laetitia*, we can see a larger ecclesial vision being enacted. In the fall of 2015, while the Synod on the Family was still in progress, Pope Francis gave a speech commemorating the fiftieth anniversary of the creation of the Synod of Bishops.[1] It may be the most ecclesiologically significant address of his pontificate to date. In that speech he explored the ecclesial principle of synodality. He noted that the word *synod* comes from the Greek term *synodos*, which could be loosely rendered, "traveling on a journey together." This principle, he admitted, "is an easy concept to put into words, but not so easy to put into practice." The synodality of the church combines two central themes of this pontificate, both of which have already been discussed here: accompaniment and listening. We see, of course, his commitment to accompaniment in his evocative image of the church as a "field hospital," a church whose ministers must "have the smell of the sheep on them." But consider what he doesn't say. Strikingly absent in his papal addresses is any sacral rhetoric regarding the priesthood and ministry. Rather, one hears a call to the church's ministers, at every level of ecclesial life, to go out and meet people, attentive to their brokenness and particular concerns and insights. In his speech on synodality he called for a thorough reimagination of the church and its ministries:

> In this church, as in an inverted pyramid, the top is located beneath the base. Consequently, those who exercise authority are called "ministers," because, in the original meaning of the word, they are the least of all. It is in serving the people of God that each bishop becomes, for that portion of the flock entrusted to him, *vicarius Christi*, the vicar of that Jesus who at the Last Supper bent down to wash the feet of the Apostles. And in a similar perspective, the Successor of Peter is nothing else if not the *servus servorum Dei*.[2]

As an aside, his choice here to associate the christological character of presbyteral and episcopal ministry with Jesus's washing of feet, rather than its more typical association with the institution of the Eucharist, is suggestive of a quite different trajectory for theological reflection on ordained ministry. But that's a different talk.

The second theme embedded in the pope's understanding of ecclesial synodality is that of "listening." Appeals to ecclesial listening may seem rather unremarkable. After all, I've never met a leader who didn't think that he or she was a good listener. Yet, according to Clemens Sedmak, Francis has made listening a central "epistemic practice" in the church. By this he means that the pope is inviting the church to see attentive listening as a patient and painstaking exercise in theological discovery, a privileged process by which we access the truth God wishes to share with us.[3]

Francis has, on several occasions, called for the concrete implementation of ecclesiastical structures and consultative mechanisms at every level of church life. In *Evangelii Gaudium*, he wrote, "The bishop...will have to encourage and develop the means of participation proposed in the Code of Canon Law, and other forms of pastoral dialogue, out of a desire to listen to everyone and not simply to those who would tell him what he would like to hear" (no. 31). What is most welcome in this text is not the call for consultative structures; rather, it is the recognition that the fruit of consultation must not be sanitized. Authentic ecclesial consultation entails more than gathering together safe voices into an ecclesiastical echo chamber. I suspect that most bishops and pastors—for that matter, most provincials, university presidents, deans, department chairs, and corporate CEOs—think that they are consultative just because they seek out the opinions of others. Yet the pope rightly insists that authentic ecclesial consultation within a synodal church, a consultation that aspires to be more than a pragmatic public relations maneuver, must attend to a wide range of voices, including those who bring harsh criticism and disagreement. *Amoris Laetitia* is both the fruit of that kind of listening and an invitation for that listening to continue as we seek to implement its vision.

In his recent book *Prophetic Obedience*, Bradford Hinze contends that there is a conflictual or agonistic dimension of Christian life that has been too little acknowledged in ecclesiology. An overly romantic ecclesiology, and this is one of the real dangers attendant on certain forms of communion ecclesiology, privileges ecclesial harmony to such an extent that conflict and complaint are occluded from theological reflection. Hinze argues that the discernment of the *sensus fidelium*, for example, must be widened to include the laments, conflicts, and disappointments of God's people.[4]

In *Evangelii Gaudium* we find in a passage exploring the dynamics of a healthy society echoes of what Francis expects from a synodal church. He writes,

> Here our model is not the sphere, which is no greater than its parts, where every point is equidistant from the centre, and there are no differences between them. Instead, it is the polyhedron, which reflects the convergence of all its parts, each of which preserves its distinctiveness. Pastoral and political activity alike seek to gather in this polyhedron the best of each. There is a place for the poor and their culture, their aspirations and their potential. *Even people who can be considered dubious on account of their errors have something to offer which must not be overlooked.* (nos. 236, italics mine)

During a recent visit to Australia, I was on a panel with Archbishop Mark Coleridge of Brisbane. The archbishop outlined a bold plan, recently approved by the Australian bishops, to hold a plenary council for the entire church of Australia in 2020. It would be only the fifth in that church's history and the first in almost eighty years. When, as a participant on the panel I was asked to comment on the plan for a plenary council, I noted that the proposal held both tremendous promise and considerable risk. If the council were conducted in keeping with Francis's spirit of synodality, it could be a transformative ecclesial event. Such a council would provide a space for patient listening. This listening would be attuned to the wisdom of God's people, but it would also give space and time for lament and even protest, however messy. It might well include a ritual expression of repentance for the failings of church leadership amid that country's horrific clerical sexual abuse scandal. Such a council might do much to reverse the tide of public opinion in Australia and bolster morale within the Australian Catholic church. However, if it is conducted as an ecclesiastical showpiece in which its leaders are determined to "move on from the past" and "stay positive," then it might well set back the Australian church for decades.

By way of conclusion, let me simply say that in its determination, both to accompany people in the messiness of their lives and to listen to people's insights and concerns, *Amoris Laetitia* is not just the fruit of two synodal assemblies, it is an apt reflection of, and for, a synodal church. For this rich document invites us to see the wisdom of listening before speaking, learning before teaching, praying before pronouncing. For only out of the deep humility of a truly synodal church can the good news of Jesus Christ reverberate with clarity and power before a world hungry for a word of hope and an offer of salvation.

NOTES

1. Pope Francis, "Address at Commemorative Ceremony for the Fiftieth Anniversary of the Synod of Bishops," October 17, 2015. The text of this speech can be accessed at http://saltandlighttv.org/blogfeed/getpost.php?id=66497&language=en.

2. Ibid.

3. Clemens Sedmak, *A Church of the Poor: Pope Francis and the Transformation of Orthodoxy* (Maryknoll, NY: Orbis, 2016).

4. Bradford Hinze, *Prophetic Obedience: Ecclesiology for a Dialogical Church* (Maryknoll, NY: Orbis, 2016).

PANEL V

The Challenges of *Amoris Laetitia* to Theologians and Pastors

16

What Theological Resources Did the German Bishops Mine for Their Reception of *Amoris Laetitia?*

Bishop Dr. Franz-Josef Overbeck

*A*moris Laetitia has been taken up very positively in Germany. The aim to empower the institutions of marriage and family, the encouraging style of the document, and the everyday language of Pope Francis hit the heart of many people in Germany. The surveys made in preparation for the synods in 2014 and 2015 received a wide response all over Germany. The participation of the German bishops in the synods attracted great attention. The publication of *Amoris Laetitia* created high expectations for the reaction of the German bishops. Prior to the synodal process, the German bishops had already planned to publish a statement concerning marriage and family. Furthermore, the question of pastoral handling of remarried divorcees—intensively discussed in Germany for years—had been of great importance in this context, even before the synod.

What Theological Resources Did the German Bishops Mine?

Against this background, the German bishops intended to foster a deepened reception and an application of the propositions of *Amoris Laetitia* on the pastoral situation in Germany. Thereby, the thoughts of *Amoris Laetitia* should neither be repeated nor commented on.

Therefore, after intensive discussions among the bishops, a short text has been published showing which aspects of *Amoris Laetitia* are considered very important in the current pastoral situation in Germany. This text is also available in English. It underlines that marriage preparation must be intensified in accordance with *Amoris Laetitia*. It points out the importance of strengthening support to the family as a place to learn about faith. And finally, the text emphasizes the importance of "accompanying, discerning and integrating" for the handling of fragility.

First, divorced Catholics who got remarried civilly are invited to approach their local church to become active parish members step by step. According to *Amoris Laetitia*, there cannot be general valid regulations or automatic processes for granting sacraments. Differentiated solutions are necessary that are suited to the individual case, to the individual biography and life situation of those seeking sacraments. The German bishops assume that *Amoris Laetitia* initiates a process toward decisions of conscience. According to them, the process should be assisted by a pastor or a pastoral caretaker. A spiritual process like this is always inclusive; it does not inevitably lead to the reception of the sacrament of penance and reconciliation or the sacrament of the Eucharist. It is, above all, the distinction (in Latin, *discretio*) made in a confidential dialogue. If, as a result of this process, the faithful decides to receive the sacraments, this has to be respected. This requires us not only to strengthen pastoral caretakers' ability to have such conversations, but also to strengthen the growing of conscience of the faithful. The text points out that these necessities impose greater expectations on our pastoral care. The text ends with the invitation to get into *Amoris Laetitia*.

If one now asks the question of which theological sources

the German bishops particularly chose as basis for the reception of *Amoris Laetitia*, the following five aspects can be briefly described.

THE LIFE OF PEOPLE WE MEET IN A PARISH

The reactions to presynodal surveys contributed to the findings that our theology of marriage and family must deal with. Most Catholics in Germany greatly appreciate the institutions of marriage and family. Especially for young people, it is of great value to manage a successful partnership and family life. Nevertheless, people are aware of fragility and of all the difficulties they may face on the way to realizing these aims. They want their church to provide an orientation, to offer strength and practical support. But few people in Germany understand and accept the ethical sense of interdictions. So, especially in the field of sexuality, interdictions that one cannot understand, that are seen as ignorant and patronizing, are no longer obeyed. Whoever wants people to adopt moral demands must clearly formulate his position. Furthermore, he must explain his position in a comprehensible way and teach people to appreciate his position. People regard themselves as the organizers of their own lives in a very multifarious and complex world. Therefore, they examine carefully the requirements for their own course of life.

THE REFLECTIONS OF AN EPISCOPAL WORK GROUP AND A THEOLOGICAL SYMPOSIUM

In 2012, the German bishops set up an episcopal working group to deal with the question of the pastoral handling of remarried divorcees. When Pope Francis anticipated the synodal process, the German bishops forwarded the results of their consultation to the synod secretariat as a theological contribution in preparation for the synod. The text was also published in English under the title "Theologically Responsible, Pastorally Appropriate Ways of Assisting Remarried Divorcees: Reflections of the German Bishops Conference in Preparation for the Synod of Bishops on *The Pastoral Challenges to the Family in the Context of Evangelization*," and found great approval among experts.

Between the two synods in 2014 and 2015, the presidents of the French, German, and Swiss Bishops' Conferences initiated a meeting at the Pontifical Gregorian University in Rome. The conference that took place included theologians from three countries and dealt with considerations of biblical hermeneutics with respect to marriage and family, aspects of a theology of love, and aspects of a theology of biography. The theological contributions and a summary of the subjects of discussion were published under the title *Theology of Love* in German, French, and Italian.

THE PROPOSITIONS FROM *GAUDIUM ET SPES* CONCERNING THE CONSCIENCE

In respect of the shortness of space, only a few exemplary references can be mentioned. A theological reference of prominent importance for the reception of *Amoris Laetitia* when it comes to the pastoral handling of difficult situations was the set of propositions of the Vatican II's *Gaudium et Spes* concerning the conscience (see no. 16). Pope Francis emphasized the importance of the conscience in *Amoris Laetitia* several times. That was impulse and encouragement to recall the statements of the Second Vatican Council dealing with the conscience and to reflect on their impact on the imparting of Christian doctrine. Those conciliar statements played a role in the deliberations of the Circulus Germanicus (the German language group) during the 2015 synod. So, as the council states, "conscience is the most secret core and sanctuary of a man. There he is alone with God, whose voice echoes in his depths" (*GS* 16). Therefore the conscience of the individual person is to be respected, just as the person must be educated to give faith space in one's own life. This is what we understand by formation of conscience. It happens especially when the person takes Christian doctrine seriously, deals with it, and endeavors to integrate doctrine in his life. For pastoral care, the clear appeal from Pope Francis applies: "We have been called to form consciences, not to replace them" (*AL* 37).

THE FUNDAMENTAL IMPULSE OF ST. THOMAS AQUINAS

The president of the Pastoral Commission of the German Bishops Conference, Bishop Dr. Franz-Josef Bode, addressed some significant thoughts of St. Thomas Aquinas in his synod *interventio* and during the discussions of the Circulus Germanicus at the 2015 synod. Aquinas emphasizes that each norm has to be applied to the everyday life of people and that the precision of theoretical regulations does not grant this, and therefore the situations of people need to be taken into account.[1] The fact that Pope Francis explicitly uses the argument of Aquinas in *Amoris Laetitia* (see *AL* 304) was a confirmation and an encouragement—in complete accordance with the doctrinal tradition—to emphasize the importance of a person's biography for pastoral care. Since it is well known that general norms and rules are not always distinct enough when applied to specific situations, it is not always possible for everyone to understand the exact meaning of a rule, and sometimes it is also not feasible to capture the situation in a rule. That is when human prudence is required to make the best out of the situation. This can indicate the need to modify a rule or to give preference to a competing rule, because otherwise a reasonable behavior would be impossible. Aquinas himself suggests that a rule cannot capture the complexity of a human action and situations.

Pope Francis makes this rational theory of action valuable for the pastoral care of the churches, for it reveals that prudent action is clearly not "laxism"; it is rather indispensable, when one wants to achieve reasonable goals. Therefore, the pastoral caretaker needs to act prudently—in the sense of Christian doctrine and in the light of compassion that Christian activity inherently determines.

POPE FRANCIS AND *AMORIS LAETITIA*

In conclusion, let us note the most important theological reference of the German bishops' reception: Pope Francis himself and *Amoris Laetitia*. This profound text refers not only to the tradition of the church in a detailed way, but also to the reflections of the synod. And it combines—in part—very personal reflections, thoughts, advice, and remarks of Pope Francis himself to a homogeneous statement. *Amoris Laetitia* is both a teaching statement as well as a skillful and almost elaborated synthesis. A very pleasing fact of the text is that the pope neither changes dogmatic propositions nor formulates new principles. On the contrary, he reduces things to their main issue: to the love described in the gospel, the love that should be lived in marriage and in families every single day. Pope Francis says, "For we cannot encourage a path of fidelity and mutual self-giving without encouraging the growth, strengthening and deepening of conjugal and family love" (no. 89). Where love is, there is God, and he calls us to this active love no matter the situation in which we are living. Apart from all the discussions concerning the importance and message of *Amoris Laetitia*, we should not forget that Pope Francis considers the importance of love and the encouragement to love as the essential message of his postsynodal text. The text's reflections, hints, and advice for dealing with the implementation of love in everyday life create a very personal and realistic touch in *Amoris Laetitia* that at the same time evokes the ethos of accompanying, distinction, and integration that Pope Francis demands in the same letter. The text's essence and starting point for reflection is the importance of love in the life of humankind. A lot can be rediscovered in this new, but also old and traditional, perspective.

Against this background and fed from these theological sources, the discussion of the reception of *Amoris Laetitia* took place in the German Bishops Conference. In this way we are working to strengthen our marriage and family pastoral care.

NOTES

1. Thomas Aquinas, *STh* II–II 47, 3 and *STh* I–II 94, 4.

17

The Guidelines of the Maltese Bishops

THE THEOLOGICAL PRINCIPLES WE MINED

Archbishop Charles Jude Scicluna

*T*he first theological principle behind the publication of the "Criteria for the Application of Chapter 8 of *Amoris Laetitia*" (published January 2017 by the undersigned as Archbishop of Malta and by H. E. Mons. Mario Grech, Bishop of Gozo) is the principle of affective collegiality and communion with the Holy Father. The doctrine at the source of this principle was outlined authoritatively in the Dogmatic Constitution of the Second Vatican Council, *Lumen Gentium*. The "Criteria" are an expression of and commitment to communion with the magisterium of the supreme pontiff and with the authentic Catholic tradition. Our guidelines interpret *Amoris Laetitia* through the lens of the entire tradition of the church. The fresh presentation of doctrine in *Amoris Laetitia* cannot be interpreted adequately without considering the gospel's core message of merciful love, the theological insights of Thomas Aquinas, the renewal of the Second Vatican Council, as well as the teachings of recent popes. The pastoral framework of our guidelines reflects a "hermeneutical continuity" rather than a "hermeneutics of rupture."

On a personal note, I have always been moved by the strong words Pope Francis uses when he describes his strong conviction that what he is teaching the church at this time corresponds to the will of Jesus: "I understand those who prefer a more rigorous pastoral care which leaves no room for confusion. But I sincerely believe that Jesus wants a Church attentive to the goodness which the Holy Spirit sows in the midst of human weakness, a Mother who, while clearly expressing her objective teaching, 'always does what good she can, even if in the process, her shoes get soiled by the mud of the street'" (*AL* 308). We are called to be faithful to the teachings of the Lord Jesus on the indissolubility of the marriage bond and at the same time be faithful to his mission of mercy and forgiveness, discernment and care. The guidelines of the Maltese bishops make it a point to quote the words of the Holy Father as much as possible: indeed, 60 percent of the text is formed of direct quotes from *Amoris Laetitia*. They are an expression of that *sentire cum Ecclesia* that, especially for us bishops, implies a *sentire cum Petro*.

A second theological principle follows the teaching of the Pastoral Constitution of the Second Vatican Council, *Gaudium et Spes*, on the relevance of the "signs of the times" in the humble search for the will of Jesus for his church and her mission in today's world. To quote *GS* 3–4:

> Inspired by no earthly ambition, the Church seeks but a solitary goal: to carry forward the work of Christ under the lead of the befriending Spirit. And Christ entered this world to give witness to the truth, to rescue and not to sit in judgment, to serve and not to be served. To carry out such a task, the Church has always had the duty of scrutinizing the signs of the times and of interpreting them in the light of the Gospel.

The following are some aspects of the concrete situation of the Maltese Islands and their Catholic population for which our guidelines are intended: Of the total population of 440,000, an estimated 90 percent would describe themselves as Catholic. Civil divorce (and consequent possible remarriage) was introduced in 2012 after the proposal prevailed in a referendum. Couples in "irregular" situations used to cohabitate with no civil status. A number of these couples would apply for a declaration of nullity of their previous marriages, with a 50 percent chance of success. Marriage breakdown and nullity proceedings are unfortunately often experienced as feuds between the respective extended families of the spouses, and this negatively impacts the outcome of marriage nullity cases. It is not rare to meet cases in which innocent parties have been denied a fair trial because of the refusal of witnesses to cooperate or because of a disservice to the truth in the testimony available. In this context, a number of genuine cases of marriages that were objectively null received a decision that the case was not proven or *non constare*. This scenario clearly demands attentive consideration in the discernment of specific human narratives.

The third principle concerns discernment as the search for the will of God in one's concrete circumstances. Pope Francis refers to this principle a number of times in *AL* chapter 8, especially in paragraph 300. St. John Paul II had also referred to the same principle in *Familiaris Consortio* 84.

In retrospect, one may interpret the guidelines of the Maltese bishops as an expression of the discernment that Pope Francis is exhorting the bishops to show in the exercise of their pastoral ministry. In his address to the new bishops on September 14, 2017, Pope Francis spoke about the process of authentic discernment. He stated that one of the main tasks of the bishop is to offer to the flock entrusted to him "that *spiritual and pastoral discernment* necessary for it to reach the knowledge and fulfillment of God's will in which all fullness [*pienezza*] abides."

Discerning therefore means *humility and obedience*. Humility with regard to one's own projects. Obedience to the Gospel, the ultimate criterion; to the

Magisterium, which safeguards it; to the norms of the
universal Church, which serve it; and to the concrete
situation of the people, for whom we want nothing
other than to draw from the treasure of the Church what
is most fruitful for their salvation today [*quanto è più
fecondo per l'oggi della loro salvezza*] (cf. Mt 13:15).

Discernment is a remedy to the immobilism of
"it has already been so" or "let us take time." It is a
creative process that is not limited to applying sche-
mas. It is an antidote to rigidity, because the same
solutions are not valid everywhere....

We must strive to grow in incarnate and inclusive
discernment, which dialogues with the consciences of
the faithful which are to be formed and not replaced
(cf. *Amoris Laetitia*, 37) in a patient and courageous
process of accompaniment, so as to mature the capacity of each one—the faithful, families, priests, communities, and societies—, all called to advance in
the freedom to choose and accomplish the good that
God wills. Indeed, the activity of discernment is not
reserved to the wise, the perspicacious and the perfect. Rather, God often resists the proud and reveals
himself to the humble (cf. Mt 11:25)....

An essential condition for progressing in discernment is to *educate ourselves in the patience of God
and his times*, which are never our own. He does not
"bid fire upon the infidels" (cf. Lk 9:53–54), nor does
he permit zealots to "pull the weeds from the field"
that they see growing there (cf. Mt 13:27–29). It is up
to us every day to welcome from God the hope that
preserves us from all abstraction, because it enables
us to discover the hidden grace in the present without
losing sight of the forbearance of his design of love
that transcends us.[1]

The fourth principle concerns the irreplaceable role of conscience. As *Gaudium et Spes* teaches,

> In the depths of his conscience, man detects a law which he does not impose upon himself, but which holds him to obedience. Always summoning him to love good and avoid evil, the voice of conscience when necessary speaks to his heart: do this, shun that. For man has in his heart a law written by God; to obey it is the very dignity of man; according to it he will be judged. Conscience is the most secret core and sanctuary of a man. There he is alone with God, whose voice echoes in his depths. (no. 16)

To quote one of our renowned professors of moral theology, Professor Msgr. George Grima,

> Priests are not being called to replace but to enlighten consciences. Even if conscience remains, as Aquinas says, the immediate norm of what one is to do in the particular circumstances, it needs to be enlightened. In accompanying persons in "irregular" or, as *AL* also says, "complex" situations, a priest represents an authorized person with whom one can dialogue and from whom one can hopefully receive assistance in finally deciding what is the right thing to do in the situation. The assumption here is that a decision taken in conscience would be a considered decision. Aquinas's notion of conscience as "the immediate norm" can be helpful in trying to understand the relation of conscience to moral norms in general and to those norms which form an integral part of the Christian life. Conscience can never be right, if it operates outside a normative framework. But conscience functions well as long as it does not withdraw from reality, however complex and messy it may be, and if it does not reduce

itself to judging whether or not an individual's actions correspond to a general law or rule. A reductive understanding of conscience, Pope Francis says, is "not enough to discern and ensure full fidelity to God in the concrete life of a human being" (*AL*, 304).[2]

To conclude with the words of Pope Francis in *AL* 305,

Discernment must help to find possible ways of responding to God and growing in the midst of limits. By thinking that everything is black and white, we sometimes close off the way of grace and of growth, and discourage paths of sanctification which give glory to God. Let us remember that "a small step, in the midst of great human limitations, can be more pleasing to God than a life which appears outwardly in order, but moves through the day without confronting great difficulties" [*EG* 44]. The practical pastoral care of ministers and of communities must not fail to embrace this reality.

NOTES

1. Pope Francis, Address of His Holiness Pope Francis to the Bishops Ordained over the Past Year, September 14, 2017, https://w2.vatican.va/content/francesco/en/speeches/2017/september/documents/papa-francesco_20170914_nuovi-vescovi.html.

2. George Grima, interview with *Die Tagespost—Katholische Zeitung für Politik, Gesellschaft und Kultur*, February 9, 2017.

18

Amoris Laetitia

A New Momentum for Moral Formation and Pastoral Practice

Archbishop Wilton D. Gregory

*I*t is both a welcome opportunity and an equally daunting task to be the final speaker on the concluding panel on the closing day of a conference such as this. Those who have already addressed us have looked at the papal exhortation from a variety of different perspectives. I want to use my limited time here to present comments that are driven by pastoral issues rather than academic interests.

While the Holy Father has presented a clear summary of all the elements of the church's traditional doctrine on marriage in his exhortation, what has drawn the special interest of the pastors, pastoral ministers, and many people in the Archdiocese of Atlanta has been the pastoral implications of this document. How has *Amoris Laetitia* been received by those who know the territory of marriage and family? How can we prepare future pastors to respond compassionately in light of this papal document?

From my conversations with experienced and successful pastors and pastoral ministers since the publication of *Amoris*

Laetitia, I can say that it has received the stamp of *pastoral authenticity* from those who know the territory. There are a number of factors that contribute to this favorable reception from those who are immersed in the pastoral care of families today. I will briefly describe two of those factors that give the exhortation such pastoral credibility.

The first characteristic of the document that I will mention is the focus on "reality." Early in this document, Pope Francis makes it clear that he intends to "focus on the concrete realities" of marriage and family in society today (*AL* 31). In a later paragraph, he refers to a statement in the *Relatio* of the 2014 synod that pastoral outreach to families today cannot be "*content to proclaim a merely theoretical message without connection to people's real problems*" (no. 201, my italics).

Even though the Holy Father acknowledges that he has considered his own pastoral experience in writing this document, the text clearly shows that he has also listened carefully to the real pastoral concerns and issues expressed by the participants in the two synods on the family.

In chapter 2, on the "Experiences and Challenges of Families," he notes that he will not attempt to present all that might be said about the family today (see no. 31), but the description that follows of the realities and challenges facing families today is both exhaustive in its scope and exhausting to think about!

This is precisely what all who carry out the pastoral care of families and who confront these issues face every day: the desires, needs, and problems of genuine families in the real world. Reading this document, they recognize that the Holy Father is very well grounded in the reality of family and society today.

The focus on the authenticity in *Amoris Laetitia* includes more than simply acknowledging in a general way the real challenges facing families today. There is also a lengthy consideration in chapter 8 of what might be called "pastoral realism." The Holy Father points out again and again that "in no way must the Church desist from proposing the full ideal of marriage, God's plan in all its grandeur" (no. 307).

At the same time, however, the discernment of what an individual person is capable of doing at a specific time has to be realistic. In order to determine "the most generous response which can be given to God" (no. 303), discernment has to include mitigating circumstances, limits to human freedom, individual conscience, and so on. This kind of realism in discernment, which has long been used by confessors and spiritual directors, is now recognized as essential for pastors in their ministry to families.

A second factor in the favorable pastoral reception of *Amoris Laetitia* is the "hope" that the exhortation gives to those who minister to families and to the people they want to help. There is a kind of "pastoral frustration" that comes when you have to tell someone who comes to you for help that "there is nothing more I can do for you."

Thankfully, through the expanded options for assistance in cases of nullity, more couples in "irregular unions" have been able eventually to enter into a full sacramental marriage. Most of the pastors that I know see this canonical process as the first option when dealing with many of these situations. However, for many and various reasons, the canonical process does not "fit" every situation, and that is when no other options have seemed possible. All of the doors seem to be closed.

With a powerful sense of mercy and compassion, the Holy Father writes that "discernment must help to find possible ways of responding to God and growing in the midst of limits" (no. 305). He challenges the church and its pastors to move beyond thinking that "everything is black and white" so that "we sometimes close off the way of grace and of growth" (no. 305). Where some have seen dead ends, Pope Francis opens the door to hope.

Amoris is a document that recognizes the real and serious problems and challenges facing families today, but at the same time it is a proclamation of hope through the mercy and grace of God. Every pastoral minister wants to give hope to others—hope for healing, for transformation, for growth, for integration and inclusion into the community of faith. This exhortation is a most welcome message of hope for pastors and all those who minister to families today.

Certainly, there is much more work to be done to carefully analyze and reflect on the teaching of *Amoris Laetitia*. We all know that it is not easy reading, and it perhaps may not likely be a "best seller." The text is at times (in the words of Francesco Cardinal Coccopalmiero) "dense" and "inorganic," in the sense that the Holy Father's thought does not always follow an organic order. But the focus on reality and the hope that the Holy Father proclaims are key for its continued warm reception by pastors and for all those who minister to families today.

Conclusion

"I Was a Learner There":
The Boston College Seminar on
Amoris Laetitia

James F. Keenan, SJ

*I*n January 2017, I received the proofs of an article I wrote for *Theological Studies* titled "Receiving *Amoris Laetitia*." In it I studied how other countries were pastorally implementing the apostolic exhortation by Pope Francis. *Amoris Laetitia*, in English, "The Joy of Love," released on April 8, 2016, resulted from the two synods the pope had held in previous years.

The exhortation is a beautiful, readable document that offers to help priestly and lay ministers in their outreach ministries to families. In my research, I found that in Argentina, Austria, France, Germany, Italy, and South Africa, bishops and cardinals together with theologians had taken creative steps to share "The Joy of Love" with their people. Could our bishops do the same? I wondered.

I sent the proofs to Cardinal Blase Cupich in Chicago and Bishop Robert McElroy in San Diego. I sent them to the former because I write for *Chicago Catholic*, the English-language newspaper of the Archdiocese of Chicago, and to the latter because he had sponsored an actual synod on *Amoris* in his diocese.

CONCLUSION

With his easy "lets-get-to-the-point" style, Cardinal Cupich called me the next day. "Listen, Jim, I want to sponsor a seminar on *Amoris* at a university. Would Boston College be interested?" "Yes," I said. I knew Boston College's president, Fr. William Leahy, would be very interested in supporting it, and I had some of the funds to do it as the director of the Jesuit Institute at Boston College. We would later get support from the Healey Family Foundation, Henry Luce Foundation, Inc., and an anonymous donor.

The seminar seemed that it could learn from the one held last year in Paris, which Cardinal André Vingt-Trois hosted with Monsignor Philippe Bordeyne, the rector/president of the Institut Catholique, for university theologians and French bishops to break open *Amoris Laetitia*. As we began to plan, Cupich was thinking the same way.

Mindful that much of the public discourse about *Amoris* in the United States focuses almost exclusively on the polarized views about footnote 351 that mentions the "help of the sacraments" for divorced and remarried Catholics, we were more interested in a reading of the exhortation's entire nine chapters. All we wanted was a conversation in the United States among bishops, theologians, and other experts on the papal exhortation that invited us to consider the full array of resources from Scripture and Tradition in responding to the challenges of the contemporary Catholic family. We believed that our families and the pope deserved such a hearing.

To get a right balance, we realized we needed some outside help. We invited Cardinal Kevin Farrell, prefect of the Dicastery for Laity, Family and Life; the canonist, Archbishop Charles Scicluna of Malta; Cardinal Reinhard Marx, president of the German Bishops Conference; Fr. Antonio Spadaro, SJ, editor of *La Civiltà Cattolica*; and Msgr. Philippe Bordeyne from Paris. All accepted but Marx, who sent Bishop Franz-Josef Overbeck, who, having participated in both synods, was involved in drafting the German bishops' response.

From the States, we invited Cardinal Sean O'Malley,

Cardinal Joseph Tobin, Cardinal Daniel DiNardo, Archbishop José Gomez, and Archbishop Charles Chaput, chairman of the Committee on Laity, Marriage, Family Life and Youth. All five were unable to come, but both O'Malley and Chaput sent delegates to the meeting. We invited another nine members of the episcopacy, including Archbishop Wilton Gregory and Bishop Robert McElroy, who all agreed to come. We invited twelve theologians (six women, six men) and another twelve other interlocutors. On October 5, fourteen members of the hierarchy, twenty-four "experts," and two donors arrived at Boston College for our two-day seminar.

We designed a seminar with five panels, each one with three to four presenters. Each panel would be followed by an hour-long discussion, and each would be the very foundation for the next. The first panel addressed how *Amoris* is or could be received in different communities around the United States. This panel gave us a profound appreciation of the challenges felt by families in the United States. The second panel raised the question of how the newness of *Amoris* affected the church in France and how it might affect our clergy, canonists, and families, particularly those in second marriages. The third looked at whether *Amoris* could help in the ongoing work of evangelization with women, millennials, Hispanics, and the growing number of "nones," those who self-describe as no longer affiliated with church communities. The fourth focused on synods, getting a sense of the theology of synods and how the synods happened both in Rome and in San Diego. The final consisted of reports from Archbishop Scicluna and Bishop Overbeck and with the expectations of Archbishop Gregory regarding the course of future work between theologians and bishops on *Amoris*.

These panel presentations were stimulating and prompted an extraordinary amount of discourse among all forty participants, not only in the five discussion sessions, but in the lunches, coffee breaks, and evening dinner hosted by Fr. Leahy. Of course, a lot of this was due to the prayer that accompanied this conference, at the eucharistic liturgies that began each day and in those intercessory prayers that we asked from others. It was also successful because of the generous goodwill of all those present. As one bishop remarked, "No one has the shields up." It was also successful because no presenter spoke for more than fifteen minutes. Each presenter was offering the first word on the question, not the unforgettable last one.

Five moments struck me as providing significant catch phrases for describing the style and content of our seminar. At the start of the first discussion, Lisa Sowle Cahill remarked, "It's so good that the speakers basically chose to describe the contemporary situation in terms of families, instead of marriages." Her insight was that the politics of marriage often sidetrack us from the more complicated issues of family, where questions of profound economic pressures and inequities, discrimination, physical and mental health, and other issues are so profoundly challenging. The second arose when Cardinal Farrell replied to a question by a bishop who asked what Roman document should take priority over others. Farrell stated emphatically, "*Amoris Laetitia*! This is the document that talks about the entry level of the pastoral ministry of the entire church." Third, a much-repeated claim was, "We have discovered that there are eight other chapters to *Amoris Laetitia*." The language of *Amoris* was repeatedly echoed throughout the two days, with many quoting notably from chapters 2 ("The Experiences and Challenges of Families"), 4 ("Love in Marriage"), and 5 ("Love Made Fruitful"). While not ignoring chapter 8 at all ("Accompanying, Discerning and Integrating Weakness"), Cardinal Cupich added, "I would caution us that there are other dimensions of family life that the pope treats in *Amoris Laetitia* that have to do not just with the moral questions but also the social life, the economic constraints, and the difficulties that people face in raising families and raising children." In talking about the eighth chapter, Archbishop Scicluna gave us the fourth phrase when he spoke of "the principle of affective collegiality and communion with the Holy Father." I would suggest that the "affective collegiality" that each of us sense with Pope Francis was extended to one another and that episcopal collegiality and the collegiality among theologians was specifically bridged. In discussing his synod in San Diego, Bishop McElroy commented at the end of his striking presentation, "I was a learner there." That's the fifth catchphrase. I do not think that anyone left the seminar with anything but having experientially glimpsed from one another the church that Pope Francis is inviting us to be.

Using Francis's terms like "the church as field hospital," "the irreplaceable conscience," "accompaniment," and "authentic discernment," we became for thirty-six hours a bit more forgetful of ourselves and more mindful of the papal exhortation on our families. It was a refreshing moment.

Contributors

Msgr. John A. Alesandro is a priest and former chancellor of the Diocese of Rockville Centre, New York, and part-time faculty member of the St. John's University School of Law in Queens, New York.

Msgr. Philippe Bordeyne is the rector of L'Institut Catholique, Paris.

Louis J. Cameli is a priest of the Archdiocese of Chicago and has served on the faculty at Mundelein Seminary of the University of Saint Mary of the Lake, Mundelein, Illinois.

Meghan J. Clark is Associate Professor of Theology and Religious Studies at St. John's University, Queens, New York.

Cardinal Blase Cupich is the ninth archbishop of Chicago and is a member of the Congregation for Bishops. He participated in the 2015 Synod of Bishops in Rome as an appointee of Pope Francis.

Cardinal Kevin Farrell is Prefect of the Dicastery of Laity, Family and Life in the Roman Curia.

Richard R. Gaillardetz is Joseph Professor of Catholic Systematic Theology at the Morrissey College of Arts and Sciences at Boston College.

Grant Gallicho is Director of Publications and Media for the Archdiocese of Chicago.

Archbishop Wilton D. Gregory is Archbishop of Atlanta and served as president of the United States Conference of Catholic Bishops from 2001 to 2004.

Natalia Imperatori-Lee is Associate Professor of Religious Studies and Director of the Catholic Studies program at Manhattan

College. She serves as a board member of the Catholic Theological Society of America.

Cathleen Kaveny is Darald and Juliet Libby Professor at Boston College Law School, a position that includes appointments in both the department of theology and the law school.

James F. Keenan, SJ, is Canisius Professor, Director of the Jesuit Institute, and Director of the Gabelli Presidential Scholars Program at Boston College.

Bishop Robert W. McElroy is Bishop of San Diego.

Hosffman Ospino is Associate Professor of Hispanic Ministry and Religious Education at Boston College School of Theology and Ministry.

Bishop Franz-Josef Overbeck is Bishop of Essen, Germany, and a member of the German Bishops Conference.

Brian D. Robinette is Associate Professor of Theology at the Morrissey College of Arts and Sciences at Boston College.

Julie Hanlon Rubio is Professor of Christian Ethics at St. Louis University.

Katarina Schuth, OSF, is Professor Emerita and was Endowed Chair for Social Scientific Study of Religion from 1991–2017 at Saint Paul Seminary of the University of Saint Thomas in St. Paul, Minnesota.

Archbishop Charles Jude Scicluna is Archbishop of Malta.

Antonio Spadaro, SJ, is Editor of *La Civiltà Cattolica*.

C. Vanessa White is Assistant Professor of Spirituality and Director of the Augustus Tolton Pastoral Ministry program at the Catholic Theological Union in Chicago.